Intimacies

By
Leo Bersani
Adam Phillips

16

EasyRead Large

Copyright Page from the Original Book

LEO BERSANI is professor emeritus of French
at the University of California, Berkeley,
and ADAM PHILLIPS is a child psychologist and
essayist based in London.

The University of Chicago Press, Chicago 60637
The University of Chicago Press, Ltd., London
© 2008 by The University of Chicago
All rights reserved. Published 2008
Printed in the United States of America

16 15 14 13 12 11 10 09 08
1 2 3 4 5

ISBN-13: 978-0-226-04351-7 (cloth)
ISBN-10: 0-226-04351-7 (cloth)

Library of Congress
Cataloging-in-Publication Data

Bersani, Leo.
Intimacies / Leo Bersani and Adam Phillips.
p. cm.
ISBN-13: 978-0-226-04351-7 (cloth : alk. paper)
ISBN-10: 0-226-04351-7 (cloth : alk. paper)
1. Psychoanalysis. I. Phillips, Adam. II. Title.
BF173.B4677 2008
150.19′5—dc22
2007034834

TABLE OF CONTENTS

PREFACE

Psychoanalysis seems to be about the things that matter most to modern people, even to those people who think that psychoanalysis should matter a lot less to us than it did in the past. The reach of childhood, the necessities of frustration, the significance of sexuality, the terrors and temptations of solitude and self-sufficiency, the lure of violence in human relations, the secrets kept from oneself and from others: all this is at the heart of psychoanalytic theory and practice. And yet, perhaps now more than ever before, psycho analysis has also become something, in William James's words, "to be going on from." It has become the discipline of useful errors, of instructive (and destructive) mistakes, of radical roads not taken. It is the contention of this book—part of a conversation that began nearly twenty years ago—that psychoanalysis has misled us into believing, in its quest for normative life stories, that knowledge of oneself is conducive to intimacy, that intimacy is by definition personal intimacy, and that narcissism is the enemy, the saboteur, of this personal intimacy considered to be the source and medium of personal development. Psychoanalysis tells us, in short, that our lives depend on our recognition that other people—those vital others that we love and desire—are separate from us, "beyond our control" as we say, despite the fact that this very acknowledgment is itself productive of so much violence. Difference is the one thing we cannot bear. The dialogue of this book is a working out of a new story about intimacy, a story that prefers the possibilities of the future to the determinations of the past.

It is integral to our project that something is being at once worked out and tried out—worked out by being tried out—rather than completed or in any way fully formulated (it would be odd for this to be a definitive book about the unpredicted life, a blueprint for an unknowable future). The book was written but not planned in the sense that the writing began without our conferring with each other. Leo Bersani wrote the first three chapters, and I then responded immediately to what he had written, giving my own account and raising questions to be answered or ignored. Bersani then wrote a conclusion prompted, more or less, by my response. Each of us wrote only about the things that interested us (like a conversation, the book is neither diligent, thorough, researched, nor finished); and by the same token the loose ends are left in, momentum being preferred to revision or qualification. The reader can read the book as it was written.

ONE

The It in the I

"Psychoanalysis is about what two people can say to each other if they agree not to have sex." We can appreciate the epigrammatic sharpness of this observation—made by Adam Phillips in his introduction to the recent Penguin edition of Freud's writings on psychoanalytic technique—without being convinced that it entirely covers what it claims to define. As the practicing analyst Adam Phillips knows, the analytic encounter is not quite as simple—or, for that matter, as sexually innocent—as that. While it is, in effect, constituted by talk without sex, the participants in the psychoanalytic exchange are, to begin with, not exactly equal conversational partners. One of them—the anal-ysand—is, in most cases, paying a considerable sum of money to have this exchange. He is also doing most of the talking, while the analyst's particular expertise (the result of years of training in psychoanalytic theory and practice) manifests itself principally as a certain kind of listening. Not only that; in the course of his mostly uninterrupted talk (think, in contrast, of the importance of interruptions in nonanalytic talk), the analysand, if he is faithful to the analytic contract of free association, will reveal the most intimate details of his life, both of his behavior and of his fantasies.

Formulated in Foucaldian terms, Freudian talk therapy is a massive sexual confession. The patient's "knowledge" of the therapist, on the other hand, is primarily transference-knowledge—that is, perhaps not knowledge of the other at all, but the projection onto the other of the patient's own psychosexual profile. Analysis has, it's true, come a long way from Freud's dictum that "for the patient the doctor should remain opaque, and, like a mirror surface, should show nothing but what is shown to him." While Freud himself had very little to say about countertransference, the ways in which transference onto the analyst can give rise to projective identifications in the other direction (from analyst to analysand) have been the subject of considerable psychoanalytic speculation in recent years. None of this, however, has changed the essential inequality of psychoanalytic talk. The analyst is not expected to analyze for the patient his counter-transference, as the success of an analysis depends to a large degree on the patient's recognizing and working through both the contents of his transference and his use of transference as a major form of resistance to treatment. In the analytic dialogue, one interlocutor is vastly more voluble, exposed, and uninformed (about both himself and his dialogic partner) than the other. Even if we allow for what have become fashionable disclaimers of the analyst's position as "the one who knows," what two people can say to each other in psychoanalysis is not only a function of the no-sex contract; it is also motivated, and in effect determined, by the analysand's ignorance and his reliance on a certain type of knowledge presumed to be possessed by the analyst, a knowledge intended to make the patient more knowledgeable (intellectually, affectively) about himself. All this chastely racy talk can stop when the gap between ignorance and knowledge has been if not closed at least significantly narrowed, although both therapist and patient, happy enough to have reached so much costly but life-transforming knowledge about the patient, have consented to an ever-widening gap between what the analysand eventually knows about himself and what he (and, who knows, perhaps the therapist too) knows about the analyst.

I confess to feeling pedantic filling out Phillips's brilliantly truncated definition of psychoanalysis. And this all the more so since Phillips's discussion of psychoanalytic technique strikes an extrapsychoanalytic chord. He makes, for example, the paradoxical claim that what must often be felt to be an arduous exercise of remembering and/or reconstructing a personal past might lead to the discovery that "there are other satisfactions than the satisfactions of personal history." Phillips also speaks of Freud as "trying to describe, through the figure of the psychoanalyst, a new way of being present to another person in a way that freed them—both the analyst and the patient—to think and feel and speak freely." This is consistent with Phillips's interest, expressed in another context, in "more democratic forms of analysis," analysis in which "the

4

idea of the superiority" of either analyst or analysand would disappear. I find this possibility intriguing, but, because I am also skeptical about its being realized, I will be considering psychoanalysis as an inspiration for modes of exchange that can only take place outside of psychoanalysis. If, as I suspect, psychoanalysis must be sacrificed for the sake of its own invaluable lesson, we might be tempted to remove psychoanalysis from the equation of talk without sex and "a new way of being present to another person" (a being-present perhaps independent of the personality constructed within a personal history). The analytic dialogue would be the accidental, or contingent, indicator of what Foucault called a "new relational mode." Having put us on the path of a new relationality (rather than merely helping to make people comfortable within more familiar relational modes), the psychoanalytic exemplification of that relationality could then be dispensed with. This possibility, which would have pleased Foucault, becomes, however, somewhat problematic when we consider all the other encounters in which people have decided, at least implicitly, not to have sex, and which, far from producing new relational modes, usually sustain and even reinforce old ones. Relational innovations are not inherent in the diverse encounters that adhere to a nonsexual agreement or convention. Indeed, the deliberate and unqualified elimination of a sexual goal from human encounters seems more likely to deaden than to renew or reinvigorate the relational field. For any such renewal to take place, we may have to return to the psycho-analytic version of the sexually neutralized encounter, or at the very least to an extrapsychoanalytic imitation of it.

In his 2003 film *Confidences trop intimes* (translated, inaccurately but ingeniously, as *Intimate Strangers),* Patrice Leconte tests this hypothesis. At the beginning of the film, we see Anna (Sandrine Bonnaire) walking toward the building in which, we presently learn, she expects to have her first psychoanalytic consultation. The titles are filmed against the unidentifiable background of what we discover to be a wall of the hallway in which Anna's therapist has his office. As a result of the extreme close-up of the wall's texture, the spectator enters the film by way of a failure of recognition that will be more gravely enacted by Anna a moment later when she mistakenly rings the bell of a tax consultant whose office is down the hall from the therapist. Leconte manages, not too implausibly, to get Anna seated on the client's side of the tax advisor's desk and to begin talking about what she calls her "personal problem—a couples problem" before William (Fabrice Lucchini) has a chance to identify himself. As the real analyst down the hall tells him later, William's initial silence is understandable (both psychoanalysts and tax specialists are consulted by people with personal problems), and Anna, too upset, she says, to continue, breaks off the meeting after a few minutes and makes another appointment for the following week as she hurriedly leaves William's office. At the beginning of the second "consultation," William's not too resolute attempt to identify himself is interrupted by Anna confiding in him some intimate details about her unhappy marriage (her husband no longer touches her sexually, and he wants her to make love with another man). William does manage to say at the end of this second meeting (also rather improbably short) that he is not a doctor, but Anna shrugs this off by saying that she knows and is indifferent to the fact that not all analysts are doctors. It is only at the beginning of their third meeting that William manages to say that he is not an analyst, which Anna has learned on her own when she called the real analyst to change the time of her appointment. It is clear that the sexually confessional presence of this attractive young woman has until now kept William from trying more forcefully to identify himself. Anna is furious when she learns the truth; she says she feels *violée,* violated or raped. We, like William, may therefore be perplexed by Anna's return, a few days later, to apologize for her angry outburst and to make another appointment. Anna and William will have ten more meetings in William's office.

Does the tax specialist conduct a psychoanalytic treatment—a treatment perhaps just "to the side of" psychoanalysis, as William's office is a few doors down from Dr. Monnier's consulting room? Anna and William never meet outside of his office; she tells this stranger the details of her troubled sexual relations with her husband, while the relation between Anna and William, who never use the familiar *tu* in addressing each other, is all talk and no sex. If psychoanalysis is about what two people can say to each other if they agree not to have sex, then *Intimate Strangers* would be (apart from the explicitness of the agreement) a testing of the possibilities inherent in Phillips's condensed recipe for the analytic exchange. Certainly, William's lack of professional credentials doesn't stand in the way of his seemingly effecting a cure. We can trace a certain narrative progress in the meetings between Anna and William, one that roughly corresponds to the unearthing and resolution of psychic conflicts in treatment. Anna's husband, Marc, has been impotent since a car accident six months earlier when Anna (at least according to her account), having gone into reverse rather than drive, backed their car into him and crushed one of his legs against the garage wall. Watching another man have sex with Anna will, he feels, reawaken his own crippled desires. To satisfy Marc's fantasy, Anna tells him that she's having an affair with her analyst. This double lie (she's not seeing an analyst and she's not having an affair) excites Anna (she tells William about bringing herself to orgasm in her bath after making her "confession" to Marc). The latter finally regains his potency by renting a room with Anna in a hotel just opposite William's office and instructing William, over the phone, to go the window to watch him make love to his wife. Anna, unaware of the role of the phone call in Marc's revirilization, happily confides all this to William during their next meeting. But her happiness is short-lived: learning from William about Marc's call gives her the strength to leave Marc, as she tells William the next, and last time she comes to see him. "I'm taking my freedom," she says, and when William asks her: "What about our conversations?" she answers, "We've said everything to each other." He tells her to be happy, she adds a kiss on his cheek to their good-bye handshake, and her figure fades as she walks down the hall. A terminable, successful analysis.

Or perhaps we should say two successful analyses. At the beginning of their eighth meeting William, who has been standing with his back to his desk, turns and discovers, with a start, that Anna is sitting in his chair. This is not an irreversible switching of roles. Anna continues revealing things about herself, but she also begins to be interested in William's life. Instead of becoming the dashing explorer he had dreamed of being in his childhood, William has simply taken over his father's work in his father's office in the building he has lived in all his life. A few moments later, Anna asks, "Is there another room back there?" which he understands as a question about his apartment, but which she meant as about another place in his mind, a place that has stayed invisible, locked. She helps him to open that inner door. Two meetings before the one just mentioned, she had asked William if he had to wear a tie all the time, if that reassured him. Not only does he next appear in his office without a tie; in an extraordinary brief sequence immediately after this exchange, we see William, alone, gaily dancing to Motown in the narrow hall of his apartment in what looks like the beginning of a strip-tease number. If Anna, thanks to William, as she later claims, gains the strength to end her tortured relation with Marc, it is William who is transformed most profoundly by their encounters. He falls in love with her—or so he tells, not her, but Marc—but he never speaks to her about his feelings, never makes a move toward her. Psychoanalytically speaking, he is like the excluded child in the family triangle. A cruel "father" even compels him to witness the "primal scene," an experience that leaves him so devastated he has to cut short Anna's happy account of the scene during their next meeting with an anguished "You can say everything, but I can't hear everything." William may occupy the position of the analyst, but nothing could be more antipsychoanalytical than the analyst confessing to his patient that she is telling him things about herself too painful for him to hear (or for Anna the analyst to be confessing these things to William as patient). Therapeutic goals are nonetheless reached. Anna's decision to leave Marc apparently frees William from his impossible position in the triangle of desire, and this seems equivalent to a purging of desire itself as, inherently, an impossible demand. Having engaged in what Phillips has called the "free listening" characteristic of a "democratic analysis," Anna and William have become, outside analysis, the equal partners Phillips has encouraged us to imagine within analysis. And it would seem that once she is able to leave Marc, Anna judges her un-conventional therapy to have served its purpose, and so she takes leave of William too. They've said every-thing there is to say to each other. She had never felt so comfortable with anyone else, she tells William in her phone message before she leaves Paris; they could speak freely, without cheating, without lying. "I'm no longer a little girl, thanks to you," she adds in what a real analyst could justifiably take as the ideal tribute to his work from a departing analysand. And not only that: this pseudoanalysis has been a double analysis, a therapeutic two-for-one. It's as if Anna had made herself desirable to William not to satisfy or to frustrate his desire, but rather to use it as the disposable catalyst for making him into a new man—less rigid, less mechanically professional, more at east with himself.

There is, however, the film's enigmatic ending. William also leaves Paris, and he manages to find Anna somewhere in the south of France, where she is teaching ballet. He sends her a note identifying himself as someone with something to return to her (it's the lighter—a gift from her father that she had left in his office), she comes to the apartment where he has set up offices as a tax lawyer, and they happily renew their old conversations. But why? Had they re-ally not said everything to each other, is this their second chance to say the only thing that may really have mattered, and that they had missed? Were Anna's long, silent looks at William an invitation, an encouragement he had failed to pick up? Such questions, irrelevant as I think they are, are of course the easiest way to make sense of the film. It would be about missed love, and the psychoanalytic conceit may have been just that, an original device to start two people on the way to intimacy, to thwart their intimacy, and finally to allow them to drop the analytic conceit and to be intimate. In short, a classical narrative with an original twist in the plot. They now have nothing to do but fall into each other's arms, which, however, they notably fail to do. And if this is what we and they have more or less been secretly expecting throughout the film, we may applaud the American critic who faulted *Intimate Strangers* for never reaching what would have been its natural and desirable sexual climax. The originality of Leconte's film is, however, to make such expectations—perhaps any expectations—and their climax irrelevant. The question then becomes, what would it be like to actively expect nothing to take place? *Intimate Strangers* violates the conventions of both narrative filmmaking and narrative psychoanalysis by exacerbating a suspense it fails to end. Is suspense the empty meaning of the film?

I will prolong whatever suspense *I* may have raised in asking these questions by making a long detour. During their twelfth meeting, Anna takes a book from one of William's shelves, reads its title aloud—*The*

Beast in the Jungle—and asks William if it's a story about Africa, with wild animals. He tells her that it is about "grey, melancholy people" in London. She borrows the book, and when she returns on her next and last visit, she says that although she found the story "very moving," it isn't her sort of book—a judgment that seems to have something to do with its sad ending: "ça finit mal." (She is, after all, about to start out for another, happier beginning.) There are a couple of other literary allusions in *Intimate Strangers,* but this one is, so to speak, negatively privileged. Anna and William will have both read *The Beast in the Jungle,* but it is referred to only briefly and in the vaguest terms; its author, Henry James, is never mentioned. Why is this the book Anna "happens" to pick out, why does Leconte have her not merely ask about the story but take it home to read, and why is there even this much attention to a book a good number of the film's viewers will surely fail to recognize? It is as if something important to the film were casually dropped into the film without anything to help the spectator identify the nature of its importance. Leconte gives us a title, and because he gives us almost nothing else, while giving both his protagonists intimate knowledge of the story, he could be imagined as teasing us into an extrafilmic investigation, which would naturally consist of a reading (or, in some cases, a rereading) of our own.

The Beast in the Jungle is, like *Intimate Strangers,* about a *confidence intime.* During a reception at a grand old English home, John Marcher recognizes, without being able to place, the young woman (a poor relative of the home's owners) who is showing the treasures of the house to the guests. They begin to talk, and she reminds him that ten years earlier, in Naples, they had met and Marcher had told her the great secret of his life. "You said," she reminds him, "you had had from your earliest time, as the deepest thing within you, the sense of being kept for something rare and strange, possibly prodigious and terrible, that was sooner or later to happen to you, that you had in your bones the foreboding and the conviction of, and that would perhaps overwhelm you." Marcher confides that this "something" hasn't yet come, and he specifies, "Only, you know, it isn't anything I'm to do, to achieve in the world, to be distinguished or admired for." And when May Bartram asks, "It's to be something you're merely to suffer?" he answers, "Well, say to wait for—to have to meet, to face, to see suddenly break out in my life; possibly destroying all further consciousness, possibly annihilating me; possibly, on the other hand, only altering everything, striking at the root of all my world and leaving me to the consequences, however they shape themselves." Marcher has told his secret to no one else, and Miss Bartram has told no one what he had confided in her. The outcome of their exchange is that he asks her not to leave him now, to share with him the haunting apprehension he lives with day by day, to "watch" with him. May Bartram agrees to this, and for many years they do exactly that together: they wait for that something lying in wait for him, James writes, "like a crouching beast in the jungle."

Over the years, John Marcher and May Bartram will spend considerable time together, visiting museums, talking about Italy, going about ten times a month to the opera, having late suppers at her newly acquired London home. What they are waiting for fails to come; there is, however, a talk that Marcher comes to think of as having made a "date" in their waiting, a talk in which it becomes clear to him that May is "keeping something back," that she "knows what's to happen." She admits as much before dying from what James identifies only as "a deep disorder in her blood." She knows, but, she insists, he mustn't: "'Don't know—when you needn't,' she mercifully urges. 'You needn't—for we shouldn't...'" "'It's too much,'" is her final sibylline reference to Marcher's inescapable and apparently horrible fate.

Knowledge does, however, come—or so it would seem. "Isn't what you describe," Miss Bartram asks Marcher in the course of their first meeting again, "perhaps but the expectation—or at any rate the sense of danger, familiar to so many people—of falling in love?" Marcher acknowledges that what's in store for him may be "no more than that." However, he has been in love, or so he claims, and "It wasn't strange. It wasn't what my affair's to be." May, apparently, isn't convinced; if it hasn't been overwhelming, she says (without insisting), then it hasn't been love. Indeed, what we are led to believe is that Marcher's great "affair" does have something to do with being in love, and that this is what May comes to know. But James keeps us from knowing this with absolute certainty until the final page of *The Beast in the Jungle,* although he does, at one point, violate his center-of-consciousness method so that we may guess that May Bartram is in love with Marcher. The latter is *The Beast'*s center; in the passage I'm about to quote. James steps in to give us an account of May Bartram that Marcher would have been unable to provide. Speaking of their having grown old together, and of their having successfully passed themselves off to "the stupid world" as a couple about whom there was nothing more to be said than that they were a couple, James adds, "behavior had become for her, in the social sense, a false account of herself. There was but one account of her that would have been true all the while, and that she could give straight to nobody, least of all to John Marcher. Her whole attitude was a virtual statement, but the perception of that only seemed called to take its place for him as one of the many things necessarily crowded out of his consciousness." The virtual is, I will argue, a central concept for the understanding of James's story, although not in the comparatively simple sense in which it appears to be used here. The point of view in the sentences just quoted is not May Bartram's; it is omniscient but selective. James tells us that Marcher fails to see the "statement" in question, and, since he is the last person in the world to whom she can give it straight, we may conclude that, although James doesn't give it straight to us, May's statement about herself concerns Marcher, more specifically her love for him.

What May presumably comes to know is that the "crouching beast" is Marcher's failure to make the possibility of their love a reality, to recognize her "virtual statement" by complementing it, and articulating it, with a reciprocal statement of his own. So when May, just before her death, rises from her chair, old, frail, and ill, but with a "cold charm" that "was for the minute almost a recovery of youth," and when, simply waiting, she assures him that "it's never too late," he sees that "she had something more to give to him," something he identifies as "the truth," a truth they had spoken of as "dreadful," but which she now presents to him as "inordinately soft." Her contact was "imponderably pressing," but he meets her invitation—her "encouragement," James calls it—with nothing more than an expectant stare. James's brief description of Marcher's failure to respond is the only awkward sentence in this moving and beautiful passage: "She only kept him waiting, however; that is he only waited." It is, then, just because nothing has come to pass that Miss Bartram can tell her friend during their next and final meeting: "You've nothing to wait for more. It has come." Marcher himself will learn what has befallen him only much later, during the visit to May's grave, which ends the story. In the ravaged features of another man, another mourner, Marcher recognizes, with envy, an "image of scarred passion," of a passion that had never touched him, and that, as James writes in the only banal comment of this remarkable work: "He had seen outside of his life, not learned it within, the way a woman was mourned when she had been loved for herself." "The answer to all the past" is that "she was what he had missed." His exceptional and monstrous fate had been to do nothing but wait. May had lived; "who could say now," James specifies, "with what passion—since she had loved him for himself," whereas he—and James seems willing to conclude his story with this strangely flat moral—"had never thought of her ... but in the chill of his egotism and the light of her use." The beast had sprung when he failed to guess why, "pale, ill, wasted, but all beautiful, and perhaps even then recoverable, [May Bartram] had risen from her chair to stand before him." And it will spring once more, this time as a "hideous hallucination" that will "settle him" in his very attempt to avoid it by flinging himself face down on May's tomb.

From the perspective of this reading of *The Beast in the Jungle* as a story of missed passion, John Marcher becomes one of James's least interesting and least appealing characters. The most charitable thing that could be said about him is that his obsessive sense of "being kept for something rare and strange" makes him the "harmless lunatic" May generously says he is not. More serious is that this little lunacy makes him boundlessly egotistical (his frequent self-reminders that May has a life of her own notwithstanding). His first thought when he realizes that she may be fatally ill is of the "loss" she will suffer if she dies before knowing what his special fate was to be. Marcher's at once grandiose and childish fantasy about himself would, presumably, be corrected, and avoided, were he to recognize and reciprocate the love that May Bartram offers him. The most interesting aspect of this reading lies in the connection James and his characters make between love and social conformity. Marcher and May joke about her helping him "to pass for a man like another," by which they mean a man attached to, and always seen about town with, a particular woman. Before knowing May Bartram, Marcher had hidden behind what James calls good "though possibly ... rather colourless manners"; with her, he becomes even more "indistinguishable from other men." "A long act of dissimulation," of wearing "a mask painted with the social simper," assimilates him to "the stupid world." Marcher and May Bartram are, however, superior to the world only as long as their real selves lie hidden behind the social simpler. If the reality they have been watching for turns out to be the failure to have the intimacy they present to the world, Marcher's awful fate, his unenviable privilege, has been simply not to live as society would have expected him to live, that is, in an uncomplicated conformity to the requirements of the social simper.

He recognizes some of the painful consequences of this failure just before and just after May's death. The stupidest fourth cousin, as he puts it, can put forth more rights than he can. "A woman might have been, as it were, everything to him, and it might yet present him in no connection that any one seemed held to recognize." He finds "strange beyond saying ... the anomaly of his lack ... of producible claim." In the eyes of society, their relation might as well not have existed as long as it could not be legitimated by any such claims, and what better claim might Marcher have produced than their having married? Their secret has constituted, for them, their superiority to a world they mock while following some of its forms. But by not having embraced what is perhaps its principal form—marriage—Marcher finds himself in the unhappy position of some one unable to "profit" (his word) from the merely "common doom" of losing the person on whom his life has come to depend. In this admittedly harsh reading of *The Beast in the Jungle,* its depressing double lesson would be first, the platitude that nothing is more reprehensible than not loving another "for herself," and, second, that the institutional correlatives of such a morally and psychically "right" way of loving are the necessary, the invaluable guarantees of self-validation. The social Beast violently "settles," hurls into a one-way intimacy with death a man who has failed to seize the opportunity society offers, through the recognized love of another, of legitimating his own existence.

James, however, seems nearly as unsatisfied as I am with this reading. There is, first of all, the peculiar rhetorical inflation of Marcher's self-discovery on the final page of the story. "The fate he had been marked for he had met with a vengeance—he had emptied the cup to the lees; he had been the man of his time, the man, to whom nothing on earth was to have happened." Why "the man"? Why is he, so assuredly, the only man of his time to whom nothing had happened? Is a missed passion the equivalent of nothing taking place in the time of a man's life? Marcher has in fact lived according to what James and his protagonists refer to as a law, a law irreducible to the sentimental moral fable of a man finally punished by, and for, his not having loved a woman "for herself." "One's in the hands of one's law—there one is," Marcher says during the talk that would mark a date in his and May's relation; and the last time they meet she tells him, "with the perfect straightness of a sybil," that his fate has already come, his law "has done its office. it has made you its own." The law uses Time (capitalized when James juxtaposes it with the law of Marcher's fate) to imprint itself on existent being: "it was in Time that he was to have met his fate..., it was in Time that his fate was to have acted." James doesn't say that Marcher's fate "acted" in the time of his life, which would have made his fate coterminous with, or the sum of, Marcher's behavior in time. He doesn't even say that Marcher's fate "was to act," or that "it was in time that he would meet his fate."

Rather, his fate is temporalized as both prior to and subsequent to its happening, as if it were a kind of being, or a form of law, inherently incompatible with the very category of happening. We have here an extreme example of those devices by which James empties his stories of any actual, or actualized content. I'm thinking of the way what presumably takes place in a Jamesian fiction is reduced to mere hypotheses about it in all those sentences beginning with "It was as if..." Also, the omnipresent Jamesian pluperfect makes of the conventional narrative past nothing more than an empty perspective on what presumably took place within that past; it pushes all taking place further back, into an unspecified beforeness. Or the taking place is projected in the other direction, toward a future in which it is absorbed into a character's retrospective reflection on it. James's characters are repeatedly taking the full measure of things (things inseparable from the appreciative consciousness in which they are embedded) "afterwards"; what James says of his heroine in *The Wings of the Dove* could be said of nearly all his centers: "Milly was forever seeing things afterwards."

It's true that in the passage I quoted a moment ago on the relation between Marcher's fate and Time, James goes on to change the resonance of these remarks in a way that makes them consonant with the psychological explanation given in the work's final pages. He speaks of "failure" as having taken place when there are no longer any possibilities in one's life, when there is no longer any time for something to happen: "It was failure not to be anything." But the notion of failure is irrelevant to a life that never really is, that is lived entirely as that which still is to be. In a few bizarre sentences, James uses the verb "to be" in both an ontological and preontological sense. Speaking of Marcher's distress at the idea of Miss Bartram's dying before their waiting is rewarded, James writes, "She had been living to see what would be to be seen." Should we read this as what would have to move into the real—to be in this sense—in order to be seen, or as what would always be yet to happen, what would never move beyond the "was to be"? Just before May's death, Marcher "bends his pride" to accept his long awaited fate as nothing more "rare and distinguished" than his losing her, and James summarizes his protagonist's sense of the accomplished in the nearly unintelligible "something had been, as she had said, to come." It's as if Marcher's fate had had its special being before any locatable time, had been perhaps always already "there," but there is only an interminably prolonged prospect, remotely past and indefinitely future. Finally, May herself, whom we might think of as advancing the argument I'm now dismissing of a definable and even precisely dated catastrophe (Marcher's failure to make of his special truth something "inordinately soft" by returning her love), May, during their last meeting, not only speaks of Marcher's fate as "past" or "behind," but, more significantly, of its very presence in the past as being its mere potentiality: "Before, you see," she instructs Marcher, "it was always to come. That kept it present." In other words, it didn't really happen the time before this last meeting, when Marcher had his final chance to prevent it from happening; its presence always depended on its never yet happening.

My "it," like James's, has become somewhat enigmatic. There are at least three more or less indeterminate uses of "it" in *The Beast in the Jungle.* There are the "its" with determinable nominal referents, although we often have to search for the referent two or three sentences back; we are momentarily stuck with a freefloating pronominal signifier. Then there is the vaguely comprehensive "it"—favored by James here and elsewhere—used to allude to the general state of affairs with which the narration has just been concerned, that is, more or less to everything and to nothing in particular. The "it" in these cases subordinates the everything and the nothing to the effects they will produce, as in: "What it presently came to in truth was," and "It was all to have made, none the less, as I have said, a date." Finally, the most heavily loaded yet at the same time the emptiest "it" refers, of course, to the unnameable catastrophe or law that Marcher and May Bartram grow old together watching for. Her first allusion to the secret he had confided to her years before provides the occasion for a brief passage that initiates us to the at times dizzying proliferation of various types of "its" in the entire text (and let's add to the list the first "it" here, a wholly nonreferential, purely introductory "it": "It took him but a moment, however, to feel it [her allusion to what he had told her in Naples] hadn't been [a mistake], much as it had been a surprise. After the first little shock of it her knowledge on the contrary began, even if rather strangely, to taste sweet to him. She was the only other person in the world then who would have it, and she had had it all these years, while the fact of his having breathed his secret had unaccountably faded from him."

The Beast in the Jungle thematizes the Jamesian tendency to extract all events, as well as all perspectives on them, from any specified time, and to transfer them to a before or an after in which they are derealized in the form of anticipations or retrospections. The designation of Marcher as a colorless figure aptly describes what is most original about him: he is the embodiment of a refusal of all embodiment. When James writes that confronted with May Bartram's "inordinately soft" invitation to love her, "he only waited," he is at once exposing Marcher's blamable aspect as a psychological individual, at the same time as he is concisely defining his character's ontological distinction: that of existing only in a mode of expectancy. May Bartram's "whole attitude" is a "virtual statement" only in the sense that she withholds the most important truth about her, her love for Marcher. John Marcher, on the other hand, is a virtual statement—and of nothing in particular. He is a life lived as pure virtuality—at least until the moment when he loses this rare dignity by speaking of it as if it were an affective and moral failure.

There is an "it" in Marcher's "I," an "it" that will return us to Leconte's nonpsychoanalytic use of the analytic encounter in *Intimate Strangers.* The new Penguin translations of Freud translate *das Es,* accurately, as "the It." James Strachey's Latinizing of the term as the *Id* in the standard edition of Freud's work improperly removes it from ordinary language, and in so doing it misses its flat neutrality. *Das Es,* Freud tells us, is the repository of repressed sexual impulses; the word itself, however, both in German and in its precise English translation, suggests something beyond, or, more accurately, before all characterization. The It is unconscious not because (or not only because) it is the hiding place of the repressed; rather, the unconscious It, lodged within a subject that it vastly exceeds, is the reservoir of possibility, of all that might be but is not. Lacan places the unconscious as between perception and consciousness, an intriguing alternative to the more orthodox view of the unconscious in depthpsychology as behind or below consciousness. One way of understanding this (which may not have been Lacan's intention) is to think of the unconscious as before consciousness—in the sense of an ontological rather than a temporal anteriority. The It in the I transforms subjecthood from psychic density into pure potentiality, the unrealized being of John Marcher's waiting, his at once empty and infinitely rich suspense.

We might take Marcher to be an emblem of art. Writers, painters, filmmakers frequently move in their late work not toward a greater density of meaning and texture, but rather toward a kind of concentrated monotony that designates a certain negativizing effect inherent in the aesthetic. I'm thinking—to mention just a few examples at random—of Turner's nearly monochromatic late seascapes, the almost imperceptible variations within the dark coloring of the walls in the Rothko Chapel, the willed thinness of Beckett's last fictions (especially *Worstward Ho),* the nearly subjectless banality of Flaubert's *Bouvard and Pécuchet,* the relentless reduction of variegated actual behavior to abstract laws of behavior in Proust's *La Fugitive,* the erasure of abstraction itself in Mallarmé's obsessively present *page blanche,* and of course the at times staggering thinness of meaning in James's late novels. The climactic sense of *The Wings of the Dove* is Densher's ascetic love for the words Milly addressed to him in the letter, destroyed by Kate, that he will never see. He will never know more than what she might have said to him (but that, as Kate sees, now supersedes his love for her, Kate), and so he will live in the stillness of a past reduced to mere but limitless wondering about the past, just as Marcher lies still during his entire life, wondering about a fate that never was and never can be more, or less, than that which was to have been. This is the virtuality of art which, even when it designates or portrays specific human figures or particular places and acts, has already removed them from the field of actual designation. Represented happening in art, however meticulously detailed, is inherently unspecifiable happening.

There is, I have been suggesting, a mode of talk outside art that is analogous to the phenomenological blankness of art, a verbal play with the unspecifiable It of pure potentiality. The analytic exchange is psychoanalysis's brilliant discovery of a relational context that needs, indeed allows for nothing more than virtual being. Perhaps Leconte saw in *The Beast in the Jungle* something like the relation between William and Anna. May Bartram's home is not an analytic office, but over a period of years she receives in her home a man with whom she has talk without sex, and the talk is centered on a hidden It that defines him. "How shall I ever repay you?" Marcher comes to ask quite appropriately, since May has performed the invaluable service of listening for which analysts, unlike poor Miss Bartram, exact handsome prices. Leconte, however, for all the interest and perhaps even inspiration he may have found in James's story, corrects its ending. James retreats from the remarkable singularity of his story (much as psychoanalysis retreated into a depth psychology from its discovery of the impersonal dimension of psychic being) by specifying Marcher's "it" as the reprehensible failure to add passion to talk. By staying within talk, Anna and William test the possibility of a de-profes-

[handwritten margin notes: de-professional / yes, radical / our models / outside of / psychoanalysis etc. / — dialogical approach —]

sionalizing and perhaps subsequent universalizing of the conditions of an analytic exchange. In so doing, they would remain true to the spirit of that exchange while demedicalizing it, stripping it of therapeutic aims. The impersonal intimacy of the psychoanalytic dialogue, the intimate talk without sex, might be re-experienced as an intimacy without passion. In their reliance on the psychoanalytic setting, Anna and William must first of all divest themselves of the psychological duress of the "real" analytic exchange. They have to endure the sexual—its conflicts, frustrations, jealousy, the drama of misaimed desire endemic to the sexual relation ("There is no sexual relation," Lacan famously said)—to emerge on the other side of the sexual. But where is that?

Purged of their sexual selves—which, psychoanalytically conceived, necessitates a purging of their psychological selves—they will now resume their conversations. Their meeting in the south of France is a resumption, but the newness of the setting—especially the open vistas, the bright light, the white walls of William's apartment—also suggest a beginning, something new. Anna asks, "Where were we?"; William goes to sit on the sofa Anna is lying on, lights a cigarette, and begins to talk. But about what? Is there really something to continue? We see William and Anna talking, but we don't hear them. They are filmed in a long shot from above, with the film's last titles unfolding against the background of William's desk, below and to the left. Only now, with their impersonal intimacy divested of sexual longings and anxieties, will they perhaps be able "to think and feel and speak freely." What they have resumed is not their mutual pseudoanalysis, but rather a special kind of talk unconstrained by any consequences other than further talk. This is, as Adam Phillips suggests, the originality of talk in the analytic exchange. It is conversation suspended in virtuality. Perhaps the therapeutic secret of psychoanalysis lies in its willingness to entertain any possibility of behavior or thought as only possibility. It aims to free desiring fantasies from psychological constraints, thereby treating the unconscious not as the determinant depth of being but, instead, as de-realized being, as never more than potential being.

In the analytic exchange—and in a relation, such as Anna and William's, inspired by it—there is perhaps the discovery of a love freed from demand. Having denied the existence of a sexual relation, Lacan, in book 20 of the Seminar, makes an astonishing claim: "All love is based on a certain relationship between two unconscious knowledges." The unconscious as knowledge rather than desire: not knowledge of or about specific realities, but, instead, knowledge as being, the all-inclusive being that is the ground of all particular being. In the individual subject, this knowledge is identical to a hypothetical subjectivity unconstrained by either its desires or its acts. In the analytic exchange, the self-hypotheses of the unconscious are realized—more exactly, suspended in the real—only in talk. And this talk may be the only imaginable form of a nondestructive *jouissance,* the *jouissance* of giving and receiving, through embodied language, the subjecthood of others. Analytically trained, Anna and William, in the unconcealing light of their new yet also familiar setting, and no longer driven by the need to appropriate the other's desire, may be at last ready for the ascetic pleasures of an all-inclusive impersonal love.

To live talk as only talk can also produce, as it does in John Marcher, a constant sense of expectation, which can also be violated, as James allows Marcher and May Bartram to do, by ending in an act—or even in a failure to act—interpreted as the act sustaining expectancy. While *The Beast in the Jungle* retreats from its images of indefinitely suspended being—refuses, that is, to allow its protagonists to maintain and to profit from their impersonal intimacy—in *Intimate Strangers* William and Anna pick up the relational cue first given to them when Anna decided to go on with her "mistake," although, significantly, they appear to do so (even though their presence is abruptly erased from the screen before the titles end—where have they gone?) within the protected confines of an analytic setting. To leave that setting while adhering to the conditions that essentially defined it would be to test the social viability of their impersonal intimacy. Are there no other versions of this intimacy, ones that might emerge from larger relational fields? If Leconte's film finally disappoints us, it is because, having so brilliantly made the case for a use of talk that might be our most powerful weapon against the necessities, and the very necessity, of settled being, he then suggests (ambiguously, it's true), in the final image of his film, that this new relational mode can survive only if it is sequestered, if the world is excluded from it.

TWO

Shame on You

Queer intellectuals are curiously reticent about the sexuality they claim to celebrate. It is frequently said that gay culture—at least gay male culture—is to a large extent a sexual culture, and while it could be argued, as Freud implicitly did, that "sexual culture" is an oxymoron, defending our right to have sex—lots of sex, in many different, and at times surprising, places—is certainly a defense of a long if not exactly respectable gay tradition. A certain reticence about gay sex, even *entre nous,* may, however, be a necessary part of that defense. The relation between the celebration and the silence was especially striking at a 2003 conference called Gay Shame at the University of Michigan. For two days, normativity—both straight and gay—was strenuously, and perhaps deservedly, attacked, but very little was said about the precise value of non- or anti-normative sexual practices. Peculiarly, AIDS was not mentioned in any of the talks. I say "peculiarly" because AIDS became a major shame-inflicting weapon—a gift, as it were, sent from God—in homophobic assaults from, principally but by no means only, the Christian right on the homosexual "lifestyle." However morally repugnant we may rightly judge such attacks to be, it is difficult for HIV-infected gays not to be also infected by the shame-inducing judgment that AIDS is a punishment for their sexual sins. If, as the gay-shame theorists forcefully argue, shame is necessarily constitutive of gay subjectivity in a society that trains us from early childhood to think of homosexuality as unnatural and even criminal, to be stricken with a life-threatening disease as a direct result of having sex with another man can hardly fail to reactivate at least some of the shame that even the proudest of gay men probably felt when they first discovered their sexual tastes.

Of course, things have changed considerably since the early years of AIDS. The Christian shame tactic is undoubtedly much less effective than it was twenty years ago, and, all the resistance to gay marriage notwithstanding, our insistence on having the right to marry has helped to make us more acceptable to straight people by allowing them to think that we have the same conjugal dreams as they do. We should not, however, exaggerate the degree of acceptance. Let's not forget that an institution as august and as powerful as the Roman Catholic Church has officially characterized homosexual being as fundamentally disordered being. There would, then, have been sufficient reason for the Gay Shame conference to devote some time to the ways in which AIDS has interfered with the project of constructing a gay dignity both on and despite the ground of an in-eluctable gay shame. I suspect that the failure to consider this as a topic for discussion may have to do with certain shame-inducing mechanisms internal

34

to the gay community itself. A potential sexual shame is inherent in being HIV-positive. For the overwhelming majority of HIV-positive gay men, to acknowledge being infected amounts to a sexual confession: I have been fucked. Many gay men admit freely (generally to other gay men) that they like being bottoms, although a significant number of less liberated brothers may still subscribe, perhaps secretly, to the view that Foucault, in a 1982 interview, attributed to most homosexuals according to which "being the passive partner in a love relationship" is "in some way demeaning." For Foucault, gay S/M—partly because of the frequent reversibility of roles in gay S/M, partly as a result of the demonstration S/M provides of the power of bottoms—has "helped to alleviate this problem somewhat" by empowering "a position traditionally associated with female sexuality." Since the political credo of the gay men likely to participate in an academic conference on Gay Shame includes being a good feminist, they would probably feel uncomfortable publicly investigating, first, homophobic shame associated with being HIV-positive, and, second, the involuntary misogynistic shame of being exposed to others (gay and, even worse, straight others) as having succumbed to, or actively sought, the sexual "position traditionally associated with female sexuality." While it seems to me that a discussion of all this among gay men might be useful, I can also see how it could easily become politically messy.

Add to this the equally embarrassing fact (also scrupulously avoided at our conference) that a significant number of gays have, in the past ten years or so, been barebacking, that is, engaging in unprotected anal sex. When I mentioned this at the conference, I was dismissed as having bought into homophobic media propaganda, which, I was told, has transformed a few isolated incidents into a general practice. The widespread nature of the practice (documented in Tim Dean's recent research on the topic) can be easily verified by visits to the impressive number of flourishing barebacking Web sites on the Internet, as well as to the video stores renting and selling dozens of barebacking films. To what extent is gay shame both a source and a product of gay barebacking? There is of course a politically correct way of dealing with barebacking: all self-destructive, and even murderous, behavior on the part of gay men testifies—rather spectacularly at times—to a self-hatred directly and uniquely traceable to a subjectivity molded by a homophobic culture. Dangers, however, are lurking in this position. First of all, while the socially inflicted shame argument gets gays off the hook ethically, it also radically deprives us of agency in our behavior. Barebacking would show how deeply we have been injured by homophobic insults to the very core of our being, but it also shows what a small inner margin we have in excess of a shamed subjectivity. Catastrophically shamed: we are in such deep if unconscious agreement with the original perpetrators of our shame that, ratifying their judgment of us, we move on to the sentencing stage and condemn ourselves and others to death. Such considerations would hardly further the projects of those for whom gay shame serves as the foundation for gay pride. Even more: once we begin to speak of such apparently suicidal and murderous behavior as barebacking, we run the risk of tracing the profile of a psychoanalytically defined death drive. When behavior is unambiguously destructive, oriented toward an orgasmic embrace of annihilation, the ultimately malleable social unconscious (the unconscious favored by anti-Freudian queer intellectuals) becomes a weak rival to the rage for death inherent in the human psyche. We would thus return to the issue of *every* individual's responsibility for the violent impulses that are partly and inescapably constitutive of our psychic structure. We are now in psychoanalytic territory (anathema to marry queer theorists), by which I mean territory ontically prior to social inscriptions, and "beyond" such intersubjective categories as shame or pride.

And yet I don't think the death drive provides a satisfactory account of barebacking. Once we have pushed beyond both the shame-based and the deathdrive arguments, we may find ourselves confronting something rarely associated with irresponsible self-indulgence: the ascesis of an ego-divesting discipline. Let's begin with a brief discussion of someone who has been taken as the very model of nonascetic self-indulgence, the French writer Guillaume Dustan. Dustan, who died in 2005 at the age of forty, was both an exceptionally gifted novelist and, we may learn with some surprise, a magistrate in Tahiti and in northern France. He became a favorite of talk show hosts on French television (and the pariah of AIDS activists), largely because of his carefully cultivated shock value: he was always ready to defend the practice of unsafe sex in the name of individual freedom taking a stand against both the straight and the gay censors who would suppress it. His first book, *Dans ma chambre (In My Room),* a novel or, to use a term favored by Dustan, an auto-fiction, published in 1996, is prebarebacking Dustan, although it outlines the sexual and spiritual logic of barebacking, as well as its inevitability. The 150 pages of *Dans ma chambre* are filled with short, declarative sentences that unrelentingly and rather breezily describe in great detail Guillaume's extraordinarily rich (yet also monotonous) sex life. The book seems designed to confirm the most cherished heterosexual fantasies about how gay men live: Guillaume does almost nothing but fuck, take drugs, and dance the night away in packed gay discos. But *Dans ma chambre,* for all its matter-of-fact presentation of a voluminous quantity of scabrous sexual details, is also rather "respectable." There are three pages that simply list all the sexual accessories or toys that clutter Guillaume's closets; while they include such things as handcuffs, nipple clamps, harnesses, testicle-stretchers, and whips, there are no scenes in the novel that would qualify as bona fide S/M. "I am not a sadist," Guillaume candidly writes, "only a little megalomaniacal." Above all, Guillaume, who is HIV-positive, never has unprotected anal sex—or, more accurately, he only briefly has it, always managing not to ejaculate when he is being the active partner and to avoid receiving the ejaculations of the many tops who enjoy his anal favors.

So Guillaume has a wonderful life, one in which, as he says, "sex is the central thing." *Dans ma chambre* is unabashed confirmation of gay culture as a culture of sex. It justifies putting those two words together. When Freud, in *Civilization and Its Discontents,* opposes the pleasures of sex to the demands of civilization, he is thinking of those pleasures as entirely private, as removing the individual from the social spaces in which a shared culture is elaborated. Although it is almost always between only two or three people, the gay sex in *Dans ma chambre* is a communal construction. Everything in the "ghetto" where, as Guillaume notes, you can do just about everything except, perhaps, work and see your family, is organized around sex: "clothes, short hair, being in good shape, the sex toys, the stuff you take, the alcohol you drink, the things you read, the things you eat, you can't feel too heavy when you go out or you won't be able to fuck." Tireless sexual promiscuity makes for a connectedness based on unlimited bodily intimacies. In the most reflective chapter of the book (its title is in English: "People are still having sex"), Guillaume happily announces, "I live in a wonderful world where everyone has slept with everyone." For a period of time Guillaume's former lover Quentin had the same different tricks every night of the week; there was the regular Monday trick, the regular Tuesday trick, and so on. Weekends were left open for new contacts. Sex was apparently always better with the regular ones, but, Guillaume writes, "the problem is that with them you get into relations that have to be managed." Quentin wasn't bothered by that because he "is a little schizophrenic." And Guillaume concludes this brief portrait of his friend with the astonishing remark: "When no one really exists, there is room for everyone." A universal relatedness grounded in the absence of relations, in the felicitous erasure of people as persons.

Might some serpent enter this garden of sexual felicity? *Dans ma chambre*'s Dionysian delights are not exactly spoiled by the specter of HIV infection, but it has clearly become an inescapable part of Guillaume's "wonderful world." Guillaume and his friends are not, as we say, in denial: they talk about their HIV status with one another, Guillaume consoles a sick friend, and he and most of his tricks are never too excited, too drugged or too drunk to pause and don the always available condom. And yet, perhaps inevitably, AIDS infects sex with a consciousness of death. Death, however, not as a threat, but as a temptation, a lure. The monotony of Guillaume's sexual exploits—especially of his insatiable anal appetite for multitudinous penises and dildoes of the most impressive dimensions—is relieved by a narrative movement away from the sex the narrator appears never to cease meticulously to describe. Indeed perhaps the most extraordinary aspect of this account of gay sex as, it would almost seem, inherently mindless and affectless is the sexual hero's discovery, within or just to the side of sex, of something superior to, or at the very least more desirable than sex. Dustan's novel delineates a wish to die that is at once related to sex and foreign to sex, and in so doing it unself-consciously resolves the Freudian quandary of a death drive different in its psychic essence from Eros, Freud maintains, and yet, as he writes in *Civilization and Its Discontents,* undetectable "unless its presence is betrayed by being alloyed with Eros." *Dans ma chambre* gives a phenomenological account of that seemingly unaccountable "alloy." At first it would appear that the threat of death merely intensifies the sexual pleasure of unsafe sex. What interests the practitioners of unsafe sex, Guillaume writes, is "to wallow in poisonous come, to have a romantic and dark fuck," to taste and to give "the kiss of death, as they say." Guillaume remembers seeing one man come while penetrating another without a condom, a spectacle he found dizzying, *vertigineux.* The potentially fatal fuck is a powerful aphrodisiac.

For Guillaume, the excitement of unsafe sex seems to be the psychic effect of his knowing that the bottom may be penetrated by his own death. It's as if the prospect of death were in itself exciting; here, however, the excitement is being "lent" to sex, where it both intensifies the sensations of those having sex and even momentarily shatters the psychic equilibrium of someone present merely as a witness. So it may be possible to experience the excitement without the sex. Guillaume seems, as it were, to be working toward this desexualizing purification of the death drive; it is his personal ascesis. Unable to come one night while penetrating Stéphane, he masturbates after making Stéphane come. Then he lies next to Stéphane, without touching him, and closes his eyes. "After a moment Stéphane asks me what's wrong. I say I would like to shoot everyone, break all my toys, and remain all alone in the spilled blood, screaming until I die." The rhythm of excitement leading to a fantasized death parallels the rhythm of a sexual excitement leading to a sexual climax. But here the exciting "friction" is entirely mental (it is the blood-soaked exacerbation of a fatal fantasmatic scream), and what is ultimately evacuated is not semen but life itself.

Unsafe sex becomes so tempting to Guillaume that, to escape that temptation, he gets a job elsewhere and leaves Paris. "If I stay here I'm going to die. I'm going to end up putting sperm in everybody's ass and having them do the same thing to me. The truth is, that's the only thing I want to do." Why? There is perhaps the memory of the dizzying excitement Guillaume felt watching a condomless top transmit "the kiss of death" to his bottom. But Guillaume also speaks of frequently losing the desire, while having sex, to reach an orgasm; at such moments, he adds, he would like to be dead. To be done with it all; nothing exceeds the desirability of that. From this perspective, both Guillaume's excitement in his fantasy of screaming himself into death and his dizzying thrill as he watches someone else being fatally infected would be necessary to overcome his instinct of self-preservation—as if a destructive, rageful ecstasy could "trick" that instinct into impotence and assure the triumph of the death drive at its most profound instinctual level (where instinct and drive would be indistinguishable).

For all the bourgeois-shocking details he scrupulously transcribes of fisting and dildo-fucking, the Guillaume of *Dans ma chambre* turns out, reassuringly for some of his readers, to be a fairly decent fellow. He is scrupulous about safe sex, and he ends his narrative by confessing how good it was to have been loved by Stéphane. This also means, however, that there are limitations to his imagination of intimacy. There is no speculation about the possibility of something other than death, or more exactly in addition to death, resulting from uninhibited unsafe sex. The desire to spread and to receive death is enough to put an end to sex and, apparently, all reflection on sex. Of course, the ground staked out by his indefatigable drugged cruising is in itself a seductively unconventional form of intimacy. Guillaume's wonderful world, where everyone has been to bed with everyone else, is a world where no one is interested in penetrating—invading and possessing—anyone else's desire. Do you want to have sex with me? This is the limit of psychological curiosity in *Dans ma chambre,* and it is a limit consistent with Foucault's call for a relational move from a hermeneutics of desire to the pleasure of bodies. Correlatively, there is a profound shift in registers of intimacy: from our heterosexual culture's reserving the highest relational value for the couple to a communal model of impersonal intimacy.

The evolution of gay sex since the publication of Dustan's first novel includes an even more radical relational inventiveness, one Guillaume might have discovered had he stayed in Paris and given in to the temptation to go bareback. Unsafe sex means nothing more to Guillaume than acting on his frightening desire to propagate death, in himself and in others. What has happened since *Dans ma chambre* is an amazing—most of us would say appalling—efflorescence of barebacking as the defining practice of a new if limited gay male sexual culture. I say "culture" because barebacking has not only a large number of conceptually inarticulate practitioners who simply reject condoms as unacceptable inhibitions of pleasure and intimacy, but also a few coherent, at times impressive theoreticians. Tim Dean has recently completed a book-length study of barebacking, and much of what I will say is indebted to his research and remarkable analyses. First of all, let's distinguish (although the distinction is by no means clear cut in the barebacking community) between those who practice unsafe sex hoping that it will turn out to have been safe (or who are perhaps so anxious to have "the real thing"—something many gay men under forty-five may never have known—that they're willing to take the risk), and those who go bareback *in order to be infected.* (There is, of course, the important category of lovers who have returned to fucking without condoms under conditions of negotiated safety.) In the barebacking vernacular, the men who pursue infection are called bug-chasers, and those willing to infect them are known as gift-givers. Since the sex often takes place at parties at which one bottom may be anally penetrated by any number of tops he doesn't know (someone anointed the King of Loads received the ejaculations of fifty-six tops in one night), the "unlimited intimacy" (to use the title of Dean's study) of barebacking is obviously an impersonal intimacy. It is as if barebackers were experientially confirming a specifically Freudian and Lacanian notion of sexual desire as indifferent to personal identity, antagonistic to ego requirements and regulations, and, following a famous Freudian dictum, always engaged in group sex even when the actual participants are limited to the two partners of the socially approved couple. What is most startling about these psychoanalytic analogies to which Dean is exceptionally alert, to the extent that they are accurate, is that they delineate a social practice that, perhaps unprecedently, actualizes, in the most literal fashion, psychoanalytic inferences about the unconscious. It is as if barebacking gang-bangs were laboratories in which impulses and fantasies condemned by ego-censorship as nonviable were being tested for, precisely, their social viability.

We may, of course, not be overly impressed by a social viability that does not extend beyond the confines of a gang-bang. Furthermore, as Dean points out, it is by no means certain that devoted barebackers have entirely dispensed with ego-identities. For Foucault, the virtue of role reversals in S/M was that, by undoing fixed assignments of top and bottom, and of active and passive, such reversals help to create intimacies no longer structured by the masculine-feminine polarity. I think that when he told gays not to be proud of *being* gay, but rather to learn to *become* gay, he meant that we should work to invent relations that no longer imitate the dominant heterosexual model of a genderbased and fundamentally hierarchical relationality. Gift-givers have been known to become bug-chasers, but, while it may seem like a deliberately cruel parody of straight masculinity to call some one like the King of Loads (as he has indeed been called) heroically masculine, the intention in so doing seems to be wholly nonparodistic. It is a way of acknowledging the bottom's right to the most revered attribute of manhood. Also, the most articulate members of the barebacking community think very seriously of the act of transmitting the virus as an impregnating act. The title of a barebacking porn film is *Breed Me;* in it, bottoms ask their tops to breed them, thus invoking a familiar if perhaps consciously infrequent fantasy accompanying gay sex. Asking your top to give you a baby can intensify the excitement of anal sex, an effect that, from a fantasmatic perspective, makes logical sense. The bottom is thrillingly invested with women's power to conceive, and, in a throwback to childhood (and now unconscious) theories about the path of conception, the rectum becomes the procreative womb. But the barebacker's rectum is a grave. And this is where the reproductive fantasy becomes at once more sinister and more creative. Sinister because it's difficult not to see this as a rageful perversion of the reproductive process. A horror of heterosexual breeding (Lee Edelman's recent book, *No Future,* is already the classic textbook of this horror) becomes the sexual excitement of transmitting or conceiving death instead of life. It is here that we can legitimately speak of barebacking as a manifestation of a sexualized death drive. What could be more ecstatically *vertigineux* than to participate In (and not merely watch) this suicidal act that is also potentially a murder? More exactly, what could be more fantasmatically explosive for the bug-chaser than to feel the infected gift-giver's orgasm as an anticipatory shattering of his own biological life *and* the murder of the "baby" itself by virtue of the fatal properties of the reproductive seed? Violent aggression toward the other not, as Freud would have it, as a deviation of an original drive toward the subject's own death, but the two ideally, "creatively," condensed in a sexual climax.

I should add that, from a more pragmatic social and ethical perspective, this literal enactment of the death drive fully justifies the heterosexual *and* homosexual revulsed and often convulsed condemnation of barebacking. It *is,* from this perspective, an irresponsible spreading of disease and death, and it is a disastrous setback for the AIDS activism that has saved thousands of lives since the early years of the epidemic. I emphasize this just before turning to the ethical originality and the ethical seriousness of the barebacking rhetoric, something of which Tim Dean is acutely aware. Against the view of bareback sex as "mindless fucking," he speaks of it as "deeply invested with meaning." More specifically, barebacking "signals profound changes in the social organization of kinship and relationality," changes that can be thought of as serving love and promoting life. The exceptionally articulate documentary pornographer Paul Morris speaks of unsafe sex as both "insane" and "essential." Insane for obvious reasons; essential in that, according to Morris, allegiance to the gay sexual subculture requires the subordination of the individual to the culture's self-defining traditions and practices. "What is at stake isn't the survival of the individual, but the survival of the practices and patterns which are the discoveries and properties of the sub-culture." Barebacking is necessary for cultural transmission. Or at least this is Morris's rather muddled argument. It would have been nice if the right of all citizens to have consensual sex had been enshrined in the Bill of Rights (especially nice given the attacks on this right), but this is not the same thing as sacralizing sex as a cultural treasure. Certainly homosexuals—especially gay men—have a long history of enjoying, more or less guiltily depending on historical and cultural contexts, exceptionally active sex lives. While this may be, as Morris puts it, a central and defining activity, I'm not sure that it qualifies as a cultural heritage that is our duty to pass on to future generations. Having a lot of sex is, or should be, immensely enjoyable; it seems to me peculiar to make it a source of collective pride and distinction. In any case, sexual activity hardly needs to be vigilantly transmitted from one generation to the next. Human beings are never more ingenious (remember the cruising ingenuities of Proust's "inverts" during World War I blackouts) than they are in overcoming obstacles to finding sexual partners; unsafe sex is in no way necessary as a guarantee of gay male promiscuity in the future. Furthermore, it is by no means clear why unsafe sex is a better transmitter of sexual practices than safe sex; indeed, given the number of men who risk death as a result of unsafe sex, there may be fewer and fewer members of the culture to whom the honored tradition can be transmitted.

There is, however, something else that can be extrapolated from barebacking manifestos and barebacking cinema. There is another way to formulate the intergenerational connections established through bareback sex. Tim Dean speaks of a Paul Morris video in which semen collected from various sources is funneled into some one's anus. We not only see several men fucking the handsome man introduced in the final scene of *Plantin' Seed;* after the tops' departure, another man uses a blue plastic funnel in which he has collected the semen of other men to inseminate young Jonas with the ejaculate of men he has never met. (Several bottoms in these videos, like Jonas, maintain a smile that struck me as at once idiotic, saintly, and heavily drugged.) Dean calls the funneling scene a "ritual summoning of ghosts" that engenders "a kind of impersonal identification with strangers past and present that does not depend on knowing, liking, or being like them." Barriers of disgust and shame having been overcome, bareback bottoms become "interpersonal intermediaries," as Dean puts it, "communicating and identifying with previous generations of the subculture." This is much stranger and more original than Morris's pious invocation of the obligation to transmit cultural practices and traditions. In fact, *Plantin' Seed* proposes a view of barebacking wholly at odds with that invocation. The written manifesto transposes onto bareback sex a conventional view of cultural transmission. The video, on the other hand, is not about the survival of a tradition; what survives—what *lives*—is the agent of several men's illness and death. Not only does the bottom receive fluid from both those who are penetrating him during the orgy and all those who have contributed to the container from which semen is funneled into his anus, there is also a kind of communication—however psychologically and physiologically unarticulatable it may be—with the men who gave the virus to the men he has had sex with as well as to those whose semen has been dutifully collected in the Tupperware container, *and* with those who infected the men who gave the virus to all these "close" infectors, in addition to all those from a previous generation who may have been the founding infectors in this lineage of HIV-infectors. From the moment of the gang-bang to the time of the bottom's death (from whatever cause), the virus—unlike uninfected semen, which, depending on whether it is received orally or anally, may be quickly absorbed into, or expelled from, the receiver's own system—remains alive as a distinct and identifiable cohabitant within the bottom's blood. A certain community thus thrives internally, although I am aware of the oddity of using the word "community" for a potentially fatal infection from multiple sources. At the very least, the community engendered by barebacking is completely nonviable politically and socially. More exactly, the rich social bonds it creates are entirely reducible to single individuals' awareness of the interpenetration of fluids within their own bodies. Furthermore, this displacement of community from what we ordinarily think of as the theater of social relations to the interior of bodies could be thought of as a freakish elaboration into adult categories of thought of infantile fantasies about the life within us, about what goes on inside (as well as what goes into and what comes out of) the body's holes.

Nevertheless, barebacking's distorted and regressive version of community also strikes me as a model of an ultimately unfathomable spirituality, a spirituality at once exalted and unrelievedly somber. Nothing useful can come from this practice; barebacking does nothing to further the political goals of a minority community (on the contrary!), and it does nothing to transmit the presumed values of that community to future generations. The barebacker is the lonely carrier of the lethal and stigmatized remains of all those to whom his infection might be traced. He may continue to move and to act socially, but that which constitutes his most profound sociality isolates him, makes his life like that of a hermit in the desert. It is as if some monstrously appetitive god had had his way with him and left his devastating presence within him as an ineradicable reminder of his passage. We are used to seeing, and even applauding, the willing submission of entire populations to the manipulations of political power, but nothing even remotely resembling this truly evil power (the subject of my next chapter) enters into barebacking. Power has played no tricks on the barebacker: from the beginning he was promised nothing more, and he has received nothing more, than the privilege of being a living tomb, the repository of what may kill him, of what may kill those who have penetrated him during the gang-bang, of what has already killed those who infected the men who have just infected him. An intensified sexual excitement may have helped him to reach his willing martyrdom, but a momentarily explosive thrill was really nothing more than the accessory pleasure that accompanied him through his passage into something that is neither life nor death. In fact, barebacking is, teleologically considered, the renunciation of what Jean Laplanche has spoken of as the sexual ecstasy of the death drive; it is the ascetic discipline necessary in order to be replaced, inhabited by the other.

Bareback rhetoric tends, however, to be far re-moved from such spiritual depths of self-divestiture. There is the bottom's hypermasculinized ego, the grotesquely distorted apeing of reproductive values, the all-too-visible appeal of an eroticized militarism, and, finally, the patriotic ethic embraced in the idea of the individual's sacrifice for the sake of the group. As Dean acknowledges—his vast capacity for empathy notwithstanding—"bareback culture would be ethically troubling less for its radical departure from main-stream values than for its perpetuation of them." In its most radical form, however, barebacking perpetu-ates something quite different: an ethic of sacrificial love startlingly similar to the officially condemned form of Catholic mysticism articulated toward the end of the seventeenth century by Quietism and the proponents of what was known as "pure love." As Jacques Lebrun has emphasized in his admirable study, *Le Pur amour de Platon à Lacan,* "the quarrel of pure love" both continued the quietest philosophy of the Spanish theologian Molinos (condemned by the Church in 1687) and shifted the emphasis from the prioritizing of passivity over activity in spiritual life to the exact nature of the state of being, of the love, that would correspond to a perfect passivity. Central to the notion of *le pur amour* is what is known in mystical texts as "the impossible supposition": if God were to annihilate the souls of the just at the moment of death, or if He were to banish their souls to hell for all eternity, those whose love for God had been pure would continue to serve Him with an absolutely disinterested love. Not unexpectedly, from the point of view of the politics of Catholic spirituality, the use of "the impossible supposition" as a kind of touchstone for the love of God was not only frowned upon but officially condemned as it was set forth in a work by the principal theoretician of pure love in France, Fénelon, archbishop of Cambrai. What could be more dangerous than a doctrine that preached a purportedly holy indifference to eternal punishment and an eternal reward? But for Fénelon and the remarkable woman who was his mentor in pure love, Jeanne Guyon, pure love demands, as Mme Guyon never ceased to emphasize, a saintly hatred of oneself, a perfect passivity toward God's will, and *une entière désappropriation de soi,* total self-divestiture. Nothing, she writes, concerns the practitioner of pure love: neither paradise, nor perfection, nor eternity. Self-annihilation is the precondition for union with God; only those who have given their eternity to God can be the perfect receptacles for all that God, in His unfathomable arbitrariness, may will to give them. An extraordinary passage from the life of Saint Catherine of Genoa expresses very well this total absence of self from the self. Saint Catherine writes of not knowing how to go about confessing her sins. She wants to accuse herself of sinning, but she can't; she no longer knows to whom the guilt of her sins can be imputed, there is no longer any self that could have said or done something for which she might feel guilt or remorse. As Lebrun strikingly formulates the extreme consequence of Fénelon's thought, it is "as if love were 'pure' once the subject absents himself from it, once this love without a subject is settled on its object and is itself absorbed into its object."

The similarities between the theological notion of "pure love" and the dangerous sexual practice of barebacking may not, to say the least, be immediately clear. And yet both can be thought of as disciplines in which the subject allows himself to be penetrated, even replaced, by an unknowable otherness. The barebacking gang-bang has none of what we usually think of as the humanizing attributes of intimacy within a couple, where the personhood of each partner is presumed to be expanded and enriched by knowledge of the other. The barebacking bottom enters into an impersonal intimacy, not only with all those who have pumped their semen into his body, but also with all those unknown partners, perhaps now dead, with whom he has never had any physical contact. His subjecthood is, we might say, absorbed into the nameless and faceless crowd that exist only as viral traces circulating in his blood and perhaps fatally infecting him. For him, their identities are nothing more than these viral remains; his willingness to allow his body to be the site of their persistence and reproduction is not entirely unlike the mystic's surrender to a divine will without any comfortably recognizable attributes whatsoever. For those of us who insist on more personal intimacies, both these instances of pure love can, I suppose, only be thought of as appalling examples of prideful masochism. But it is difficult to locate in either case the pleasure inherent in masochism or, more radically, the subject to whom pride might be imputed. Of course, both barebacker and the proponent of pure love continue to exist, for other people, as identifiable individuals; but at the ideal limit of their asceses, both their individualities are overwhelmed by the massive anonymous presence to which they have surrendered themselves. My analogy between the two may appear less grotesque in the light of the vicissitudes in the history of spirituality. In a fundamentally atheistic culture in which religious belief has become indistinguishable from a humanistic agnosticism or has been reduced to an ignorant, intolerant and ego-driven fundamentalism, the spirituality practiced by Fénelon and Mme Guyon can perhaps only be sheltered and nurtured in such admittedly debased forms as the ethically and politically ambiguous cult of barebacking. We might, however, remind ourselves that a defining characteristic of the spiritual culture we live in is its suspicion of spirituality *tout court:* commentators have, for example, not hesitated to reduce the sublime self-abnegation of Fénelon and Mme Guyon to a discredited sublimation of their sexual interest in each other, just as barebacking can be reduced to an ingenious variation on such mainstream values as patriotism and heroic masculinity.

To the extent that it embodies, both through and beyond death, the desire to maintain an intergenerational brotherhood, barebacking, for all its ethical ambiguities, is a ritual of sacrificial love. A sign of my own troubled response to the practice is that I also find bug-chasing and gift-giving sexually repellent and staggeringly irresponsible behavior. Of course, even the irresponsibility can appear to be a minor sin in the larger social context of the murderous irresponsibility of the domestic and foreign policies of our current government. Many barebackers (not the self-confessed bugchasers) prefer not to know the HIV status of their partners, but no one is advocating nonconsensual unsafe sex. This is not to deny the seriousness of spreading the infection, with or without mutual consent, but even the most ardent gift-givers seem unmotivated by the thrill of exercising murderous power. Interpreted as a mode of ascetic spirituality, bug-chasing and giftgiving among barebackers are implicit critiques of the multiple forms of ego-driven intimacy: from the most trivial expressions of sexual vanity (bareback videos, unlike other gay porn, include singularly unattractive bodies), to the prideful exclusiveness of the family as a socially blessed, closed unit of reproductive intimacy, and even to the at once violently aggressive and self-shattering ego-hyperbolizing of racial, national, ethnic, and gendered identities.

A critique but not a resistance: the awesome abjection of "pure love" can only take place in the margins of the far more viable, inventive, and destructive exercises of personal and collective ego expansion. Might there be forms of self-divestiture not grounded in a teleology (or a theology) of the suppression of the ego and, ultimately, the sacrifice of the self? Perhaps self-divestiture itself has to be rethought in terms of a certain form of self-expansiveness, of something like egodissemination rather than ego-annihilation. To affirm, as a paradoxical conclusion to the rest of this discussion, that only the ego can love is to suggest the necessity of a theory of love—a necessity I will presently address—grounded in what has become, for me, the indispensable concept of an *im*personal narcissism.

THREE

The Power of Eviland the Power of Love

Imagine: a rather attractive man in his thirties persuades a young man he meets at a shopping mall to come home with him. Soon after they arrive, he photographs then drugs the boy, strangles him and dismembers his body with a saw. The victim's skull may be boiled for safekeeping; the head of another (seventeen male visitors are murdered) may end up in the man's freezer, while his genitals could very well be stored in an iron soup kettle. According to the killer himself, he enjoyed sex with parts of the corpses of his victims and, again according to the perpetrator of these acts, he was just preparing to eat the heart of one of the young men at the moment of his arrest.

Do we have any way to understand this behavior? On February 8, 2005, Benedict Carey wrote a piece for the science section of the New York Times entitled "For the Worst of Us, the Diagnosis May Be Evil." Certain forensic scientists have, apparently, come to think of predatory killers "as not merely disturbed but evil. Evil in that their deliberate, habitual savagery defies any psychological explanation or attempt at treatment." Dr. Michael Stone of New York University specifies: "We are talking about people who commit breathtaking acts, who do so repeatedly, who know what they're doing and do it in peacetime." Dr. Stone and his likeminded colleagues acknowledge that broken homes, childhood trauma, and malignant narcissism are common to such "lethal predators" as Jeffrey Dahmer (whose résumé readers will have recognized above), Theodore R. Bundy, and John Wayne Gacy; nonetheless, they describe these killers as "psychopathic, sadistic and sane." While we might think that psychopathic sadism would, by definition, exclude the category of sanity, the emphasis on sanity is in fact necessary: it authorizes the displacement of analysis from the psychic to the moral, thereby preserving the psychic from any traces of an ineradicable ethical stain. Habitual savagery is not a property of mind. The affixing of moral categories thereby becomes a tactic of unavowed self-purification; it sequesters certain persons and certain behaviors in a different universe from that of the moralists. Expelled from the psychic, these moral monsters are confined within the satisfyingly unimaginable and theologically sponsored universe of evil. It would be a psychoanalytic truism to say that this gesture of expulsion is a sure sign of the monster's proximity to our own psychic life. If we were already guilty of impulses made horrifically manifest in the crimes of serial killers, what better (or worse) way to protect ourselves from Dahmerism than to declare it humanly inconceivable?

And yet, to recognize our closeness to the possibility of serial killing (and, on a larger scale, of genocide) might, unexpectedly, justify an appeal to the highly suspect category of evil. Now, however, its invocation would not be a key element in a self-vindicating move from the psychological to the moralistic, but would rather be the sign of a very different sort of move: from the explanations of psychology to a psychoanalytically grounded ethic. Nothing is more absurd, Freud asserts in *Civilization and Its Discontents,* that what is perhaps the most cherished biblical commandment: "Thou shalt love thy neighbor as thyself." This commandment, revered as "one of the ideal demands" of civilized society, is "really justified by the fact that nothing else runs so strongly counter to the original nature of man," which, Freud claims, dictates not that we love our neighbors, but rather that we exploit them, rob them, rape them, murder them. Much of Jacques Lacan's 1959– 60 seminar *The Ethics of Psychoanalysis,* and in particular the March 20 lesson entitled "Love of One's Neighbor," is a gloss on Freud's profoundly disabused view of the moral law that enjoins us to love others. The way in which Freud confronts this commandment is, for Lacan, the very heart of *Civilization and Its Discontents:* "that is where he begins, where he remains throughout, and where he ends up. He talks of nothing but that."

"That," for the Lacan of the ethics seminar, is the problem of evil—not, however, an evil projected onto an alien other, but rather evil as an intractable murderousness constitutive of the human itself. If we dismiss—as it seems to me we should—the more or less optimistic psychoanalytic theories between Freud and Lacan, theories that would make us more or less happy by way of such things as adaptation to the real and genital normalcy, then we may judge the great achievement of psychoanalysis to be its attempt to account for our inability to love others, and ourselves. The promises of adaptive balance and sexual maturity undoubtedly explain the appeal of psychoanalysis as therapy, but its greatness may lie in its insistence on a human destructiveness resistant to any therapeutic endeavors whatsoever.

Not only that: while insisting on the nonerotic character of this aggressiveness presumably opposed to love, Freud undermines his own resolutely embraced dualism by recognizing the "extraordinarily high degree of narcissistic enjoyment" that accompanies satisfied aggression. Both the continuity and the incommensurability of sexualized aggression and what we ordinarily mean by sex are simply and profoundly designated by Lacan's use of the word *jouissance.* *Jouir* is the French word for coming, for having an orgasm. Lacanian *jouissance* unavoidably evokes orgasmic pleasure, but it is a sexual pleasure that sex can't give; indeed, it pushes pleasure beyond itself, to the point of becoming the enemy of pleasure, that which lies "beyond the pleasure principle." "My neighbor's *jouissance,*" Lacan states, "his harmful, malignant *jouissance,* is that which poses a problem for my love"—the insurmountable problem of an ecstasy dependent (for both my neighbor and myself)—on my being destroyed. *Jouissance* accompanies the "unfathomable aggressivity" at the heart of both the other's love for me and my love for the other; to follow Freud in *Civilization and Its Discontents* is, as Lacan claims, to conclude that "we cannot avoid the formula that *jouissance* is evil." It is this intractable and ecstatic destructiveness that we refuse to acknowledge by projecting it, as evil, on others, thereby denying our own ineradicable guilt.

We live in a period dominated by what Laplanche has called the psychotic enclaves of good and evil. Imagine: a group of men, having manipulated the political system of the most powerful country in the world so that their presidential candidate is declared the winner of an election he in fact lost, interpret this thuggery on their part as a mandate to go to war. The 9/11 terrorist killing of nearly three thousand people—a tragic but modest number compared to the tens of thousands of Iraqis slaughtered by the American military machine, Iraqis who had nothing whatever to do with 9/11—was, as many others have pointed out, eagerly seized upon as providing the moral justification for an imperialist takeover of a Middle Eastern country. The dream of this conquest had been nurtured for many years; it was fraudulently promoted, and accepted by the majority of the American people as well as by an impressive majority of their elected representatives, as a necessary move in the war on terrorism. By now, many Americans and, we might hope, nearly all their representatives know that the invaded country never constituted a threat to the security of the United States: no weapons of mass destruction were found, no credible link has ever been established between Saddam Hussein and al-Qaeda. None of this has changed the militant rhetoric of our leaders: in the face of all the evidence to the contrary, they continue to repeat, with remarkable consistency, persistence and only somewhat diminished effectiveness that the invasion of Saddam Hussein's Iraq was a noble response of the free world to the evil of Islamic-inspired terrorism. Certain supporting arguments have, it's true, been modified: if the war didn't save us from nonexistent weapons of mass destruction, it saved the people of Iraq from Saddam's tyranny and, in so doing, some-how also delivered a severe blow to al-Qaeda. Those who rule us have brilliantly applied the maxim that the best defense against truth is the unswerving repetition of lies. And perhaps their most impressive success has been to make their domestic opponents believe that the occupation of Iraq is amenable to the Enlightenment value of debate. They have led both the liberal and the conservative opposition to the war to argue whether or not it is possible to bring democracy to the Middle East. This is an astonishing development: first of all, because the dream of transforming Iraq into a model democracy in no way inspired the dream of invading Iraq, and, secondly, because a passion for, more exactly the slightest interest in democracy has never been a determinant in our relations with other countries in that area or, for that matter, in any other area of the world. We have (like all other imperial powers in human history) easily accommodated ourselves to, indeed embraced, the most ruthless dictatorships as long as they serve American political and financial interests. In any case, since we have certainly not gone to the trouble of occupying Iraq to have that country elect a government hostile to American interests (our supposed deference to the will of the people has been nicely illustrated by plans to starve the Palestinians into de-electing Hamas), we are certainly not going to allow the Iraqis (and it would be idiotic, from the current American government's point of view, to do so) to put into even puppet-power anyone receptive to the undermining of U.S. power in the country and in the region. There will always be more bombs and—although here the numbers have been diminishing—more brainwashed volunteers to come to our nation's rescue in any such terrifying eventuality.

Having moved from serial killers to government-sponsored mass murder, I must ask about the events I have just summarized the same question I raised concerning Jeffrey Dahmer: do we have any way to understand this behavior? Psychoanalyzing collectivities is, as Freud warned in *Civilization and Its Discontents,* a risky enterprise. Where, exactly, is the collective or governmental psyche that corresponds to the individual psyche? In studying the behavior of nations, we should remember Foucault's emphasis on the nonsubjective locus of exercises of power. "Power relations are both intentional and nonsubjective"; "there is no power that is exercised without a series of aims and objectives," but the latter are not the result of the choices or decisions of individual subjects. In his later work, Foucault was interested in the ways in which power has been exercised in Western societies to produce specific kinds of human subjects. Subjectivities are not the source of power's exercises; instead, they are what power aims to produce. An objective rather than an origin. Intentionality is not eliminated in the Foucaldian analysis of power; it is displaced. Another way of expressing this—which will lead us to see the relevance of psychoanalysis to Foucault's non-, even antipsychoanalytic thesis—would be to say that power aims to produce subjects defined (and, correlatively, made visible and controlled) by particular desires.

The effectiveness of this operation can, it seems to me, be explained only from a psychoanalytic perspective on desire. Foucault evaded this necessity, and made the evasion seem almost negligible, by his brilliant but limiting subordination of desire to an intentionalizing perspective *on* desire. He recognizes the importance of desire as constitutive of a modern subjectivity, but he defines the desire produced by specifically modern exercises of power as the subject's desire *to know his desire.* The peculiarity of this extended moment in the history of power (our moment) would not have anything to do with the nature or content of the modern subject's desires, but rather with the subject's acquiescing to the view (promoted by power) that his desires (in particular, his sexual desires) are the key to his being. The defining desires themselves are secondary to this epistemological hunger, almost irrelevant to the classifications and consequent management made possible by our knowledge of them. Authoritarian systems of government naturally profit from the confessional habits produced by the diffuse exercises of power analyzed by Foucault. Confession makes subjects visible, and their visibility (ideally, the visibility of desires that, they have been made to believe, constitute their essence) is a precondition of their political subjection. But for subjects to be *actively* subjected (to collaborate with the agents of their subjection), it is necessary to produce more specific desires.

Foucault saw psychoanalysis as an essentially sinister moment in the exercise of power in Western history. While psychoanalysis can certainly be shown to have served a massive power strategy of normativizing subjectivity, its very effectiveness in that inglorious role could be said to depend on the accuracy of the psychic profile it has drawn. The language of psychoanalysis has both served and demystified strategies designed to control human subjects. Its invaluable function has been to provide what seems to me a transhistoric account, at least for Western culture, of psychic mechanisms assumed and exploited by strategies of power. Its analytic and classificatory approach to the mind lends itself to both a disciplinary and a liberating intentionality. If psychoanalysis has designed a mental map that can guide projects of political mastery, that very same map gives us the terms of a reverse discourse (an aspect of power exercises that interested Foucault very much) that can be used to resist projects of subjection.

Thus the imperialist project of invading and appropriating foreign territories corresponds to what Freud calls nonsexual sadism in the 1915 essay "Instincts and Their Vicissitudes," which he defines as "the exercise of violence or power upon some other person or object," the attempted mastery over the external world. This is an ego-project, a defensive move (or a preemptively offensive move) against the world's threatening difference from the self. Freud will return to this idea of a nonsexual aggressiveness, although he also seems inclined to challenge it at the very moments it is most emphatically advanced. The resolutely embraced dualism of love and aggressiveness in *Civilization and Its Discontents* is, as I have said, undermined by Freud's recognition of the "extraordinarily high degree of narcissistic enjoyment" that accompanies satisfied aggression. Intense narcissistic pleasure sexualizes satisfied aggression. An achieved "mastery over the external world" swells, we might say, the triumphant ego. Or, to repeat

Lacan's formulation, our "unfathomable aggressivity" produces a "harmful, malignant *jouissance,*" which, I would add, is what makes aggressivity intractable. We can go one step further. Freud's most profound originality, it seems to me, is to propose not only that satisfied aggression is accompanied by an erotic excitement, that it produces a narcissistic *jouissance,* but also, and more radically, that the sexualizing of the ego is identical to the shattering of the ego. Beginning with the *Three Essays on the Theory of Sexuality,* Freud distinguishes between, on the one hand, the narratives of both the sexual act (leading up to and climaxing in orgasm) and sexual development (leading up to and climaxing in hetero-sexual genitality) and, on the other hand, something like the very essence of the sexual that would consist in a shattering of ego boundaries produced by any number of "unaccountable," unclassifiable objects. There are degrees of self-shattering, ranging from such examples of sexually stimulating situations (given by Freud in the *Three Essays)* as intellectual strain, verbal disputes, and railway travel, to the ultimate devastation of the ego and the subject in death. What all these very different stimuli have in common is their ability to set affect free from psychic organization; unbound affect produces the excitement of *jouissance.* The "extraordinary narcissistic enjoyment" that accompanies satisfied aggression at once hyperbolizes the ego and risks shattering its boundaries.

The death drive as a drive to destroy others would add very little to a fundamentally nonpsychoanalytic Hobbesian view of human nature. What is uniquely psychoanalytic (even if it has been disavowed by a number of psychoanalytic thinkers) is the notion that the pleasurable power of satisfied aggression is itself a threat to the agent of aggression. In Freudian terms, the hyperbolic ego risks being shattered by its own narcissistically thrilling inflation. Thus, sadistically motivated narcissism is also masochistically satisfying. Psychoanalysis makes a concession to categorical ways of thinking by providing different, even opposing, definitions of narcissism, sadism, and masochism, but psychoanalytic thinking lies outside categorical thought.

The most disorienting aspect of the psychoanalytic map of the human psyche is a group of unstable polarities (sadism and masochism, eros and thanatos, ego and super-ego), polarities whose opposite points, or locations, or instances, can simultaneously maintain, if only for heuristic purposes, their distinctness, and collapse into identity.

A collectivized impulse to self-destruct is, paradoxically, never more visible than at those moments when a nation or empire appears to be at the height of its power—for example, at the current moment of American power. At such times, there is, perhaps necessarily, a certain nonsexual exploitation of the human vulnerability to destructive and self-destructive *jouissance.* If what we might call the ruling ego's interests are to be preserved, that ego must remain unswollen—unshattered—by its own hyperbolic rhetoric. And yet it is just as indispensable that the egoic project of a nation's rulers be sexualized in those who will be the expendable agents of these projects. Only the rulers (political, financial, religious) have sufficiently powerful ego-interests to sustain their "sadism" without endangering it through narcissistic exaltation. For the others (the overwhelming majority), the national or racial ego must be narcissistically celebrated to the point of a self-destructive exaltation—in psychoanalytic terms, a masochistic *jouissance.* What has frequently been spoken of as the mass hysteria deliberately cultivated by dictatorships is this suicidal frenzy of the hyperbolized ego. It is inadequate to speak of this frenzy as a mere willingness to die for one's country or religion; once the rulers' nonsexual sadism has been sexualized in those who are ruled, only self-immolation can sate the latter's boundless (or, to use the word Freud borrowed from Romain Rolland, oceanic) narcissism.

Politically, this of course means the sacrifice of legitimate ego interests as a possible resistance to the rulers' projects of mastery. For the ego is not only the agency of an ultimately self-destructive will to master the world; it is also the agent of the subject's self-preservation. As such, it cultivates a critical faculty that allows it to evaluate the benefits and the dangers of the messages sent to it by the world. Psychoanalysis is certainly not—at least not in its most original and profound discoveries—an ego-psychology; and yet it recognizes the indispensable function of the ego's capacity to reason and judge in the subject's efforts to protect himself or herself from the drives—in particular, the drive toward destructive *jouissance*—that *are* the distinctive discovery of psychoanalysis. The frequently observed anomaly of people voting against their own interests is not, or is not principally, an effect of ignorance and/or stupidity (and it is patronizing, on the part of a liberal elite, to think that it is). Something more fundamental is at work: a cultivation of the superior power of the ego's suicidal self-love over its self-preservative aptitude for critical evaluation. It would be absurd to claim that our coolly brutal leaders were mapping their strategies in such psychoanalytic terms. Indeed, one of the great virtues of a Foucaldian perspective on exercises of power is that it does not require an appeal to any such subjective awareness and intention. It is not necessary to be consciously familiar with the drives explicitly articulated by psychoanalysis to operate within the field of knowledge dominated, as I have suggested, by a tension between the enlightened self-interest of ego-rationalism and the rageful drive to destroy that characterizes the ego once it is seduced by the prospect of hyperbolizing itself.

The latter project depends on the ego being taken over by that part or subdivision of itself that Freud called the super-ego. The super-ego is the death drive's agent of moralization. Politically, this means that the ego's aptitude for masochistic narcissism is officially, and collectively, sanctioned as patriotism (or the self-proclaimed superiority of any group). This is accompanied by the vindicating projection of the drive to destroy onto a different group identified as evil. "Evil" is the word that displacement of the death drive allows us to apply to others who become, in a collectivized fantasy, intent on destroying us, thus requiring our destruction of them. Freud defended psychoanalysis against its imputedly exclusive emphasis on sexuality by pointing out the importance it gives to the superego as the guardian of civilized morality. But in *The Ego and the Id,* he also insists on the intimate connection between the super-ego and the id: if the ego is the psychic representative of the claims of external reality, the super-ego stands in contrast to the ego as "the representative of the internal world, of the id." This dual, superficially contradictory function is strikingly condensed in Lacan's account of the super-ego, usually thought of as prohibitive, as, on the contrary, the psychic instance that enjoins us to transgress the Law it internalizes, the voice whose imperative is *Jouis!* In terms of contemporary religious politics, the deliberately false identification of Saddam Hussein's secular dictatorship with Islamic fundamentalism authorizes the acting out of the murderous impulses of our own Christian fundamentalism against the mirror image of itself. The self-cleansing gesture we began by noting in the relegating of unquenchably violent impulses onto the "evil" behavior of serial killers, a behavior said to be mysteriously beyond the psychic, beyond the human itself—that self-purifying move *is* the super-ego's "morality." It is as if the ego, in its conflicted relations with the super-ego, were not at odds with a prohibitive guardian of civilized morality, but had brilliantly reinvented itself as a voice authorizing its otherwise unspeakable impulse to shatter itself in its mad project of mastering, that is, obliterating the world-as-difference.

If the skeptical, rational ego is by nature opposed to the ecstasy of ego- and world-annihilation, it is also in practice a weak opponent of such thrilling destructiveness. There is very little evidence of a rational will effectively controlling the ego's expansions, arresting it at the size or stage of a humane sense of individual dignity and an equally humane respect for the worth of other, similarly restrained egos. Psychoanalysis has decisively discredited any such rationalistic dream. There is, however, another possibility: might the excitement of the hyperbolized ego be forestalled not by the rational will but by a nondestructive eroticizing of the ego? I will attempt to describe a narcissistic pleasure that sustains human intimacy, that may be the precondition for love of the other.

Every theory of love is, necessarily, a theory of object relations. Love is transitive; to conceptualize it is to address not only the question of how we choose objects to love, but also, more fundamentally, the very possibility of a subject loving an object. From the very start, psychoanalysis has been skeptical about that possibility. "The finding of an object," Freud famously declared in the 1905 edition of *Three Essays on the Theory of Sexuality,* "is in fact a re-finding of it." Love, which we like to think of as a discovery, is inseparable from memory. "There are thus good reasons," Freud writes, "why a child sucking at his mother's breast has become the prototype of every relation of love." Not only that: the resurrected object may really be the loving subject, a self we lovingly recover at the very moment we may wish to celebrate our openness to the world, that is, to an irresistibly seductive otherness. The difficulty of maintaining a sharp distinction between object-love and narcissism becomes especially clear in Freud's 1914 essay, "On Narcissism: An Introduction," in which Freud is also attempting to elaborate a theory of love based on that very distinction. Originally, Freud writes, every one has "two sexual objects: himself and the woman who tends him" (or "the man who protects"). The person who will re-present this woman later on for the exemplary lover according to the authentic object-choice model—Freud reserves this privilege for the heterosexual male—is typically the object of an overestimation, or idealization. Although idealization of the loved object might seem out of place in an essay on narcissism, Freud traces the overvaluation of the loved one back to the subject's infantile narcissism. The childhood ego "deems itself the possessor of all perfections"; once that illusion is lost, the subject "projects ahead of him as his ideal ... his substitute for the lost narcissism of his childhood—the time when he was his own ideal." The "excellence" projected onto the beloved is the lover's own excellence, one his "ego [now] lacks for the attainment of its ideal." Thus, even in the case presented as closest to pure object-love, the loved one carries the burden of being identified with two other love objects that have nothing to do with her: the man's mother and his own idealized infantile ego.

What, then, can it mean, from a Freudian point of view, to say that we should or even can love others "for themselves"? Psychoanalytically speaking, the loved one is little more than a prop for a revival of at least two other (lost) loved ones. The Lacanian view of love is a shifting, even a shifty, one, but there is a fairly consistent reaffirmation of what he calls in *Four Fundamental Concepts of Psychoanalysis* love's "fundamentally narcissistic structure." And there is this from seminar 20, given in 1972– 73, eight years after the *Four Concepts:* "love ... never makes any one go out of himself." If that, Lacan emphasizes, is what Freud meant, if indeed he meant nothing but that when he introduced the concept of narcissistic love, every one can recognize that "the problem is how there can be love for another person." (Lacan never tires of attacking those analysts—principally the American proponents of ego psychology—who ignore this problem with their faith in "oblatory love," a love to which the subject offers up, sacrifices his own needs. Their "pathological optimism"—to use Salman Akhtar's critical characterization of recent psychoanalytic theory—is, for Lacan, a betrayal of Freud.) As other analysts writing at the time of Freud's essay on narcissism had, Lacan suggests, the courage to say, loving objects—or, as Lacan puts it in more technical terms in the Transference seminar, "the investing of objects"—is something of a miracle.

From the psychoanalytic perspective most profoundly exemplified by Freud and Lacan, a theory of love can't help but be a demystification of love. Other theories of all the different types of love share one assumption: in love, the human subject is exceptionally open to otherness. A privileged object immobilizes our desire, a desire that can take many forms and that does not necessarily include knowledge or even esteem for its object. From an exclusive sexual passion (happy or unhappy) for someone whose difference from ourselves we may or may not claim to be able to penetrate, to the nonsexual, all-consuming phenomenon of "pure love" elaborated by seventeenth-century mystics as an unqualified self-divestiture required by obedience to the unknowable will of a transcendent, arbitrary God—all along the scale of love separating these extremes, the one constant feature appears to be a subject's passionate, fixed attention (an attention demanding or nondemanding, sexual or nonsexual) to an object (personal, collective, divine) distinct from himself. Since concepts of love very frequently include the idea of union with the loved object, this distinction does not imply a permanent separation between the lover and the beloved. Two different beings may be thought of as merging in the happy fulfillment of a personal love; the patriot "belongs" to the nation for which he willingly sacrifices himself; the practitioner of "pure love" aspires to an absorption in God's will in which his own subject-being is annihilated. But in all these cases union is a *goal* (even if it is thought of as predestined, as somehow, somewhere already designed), a goal that changes nothing in the subject's "investment" in someone or something that he is not. Love is an exemplary concept in all philosophical speculation about the possibility of connectedness between the subject and the world. The theory of love adumbrated in Freud and Lacan is demystifying in the sense that it subverts the premise about being on which love is founded, the assumption that in love the human subject is exceptionally open to otherness. We love only ourselves (as Lacan puts it more concretely in the seminar on Identification: "I love only my body, even when I transfer this love onto the body of the other"), a truth that explodes the myth of love.

Could the presumed truth about the inescapably specular nature of love be reformulated in a way that saves the myth? Or, to put this differently, is there a myth that might have anticipated the psychoanalytic truth about love, anticipated it not as a demystification but as a reconciliation of narcissism and our authentic being-in-the-world? Given my earlier discussion, the stakes are high: I will be asking whether the power of evil might be defeated, or at least eluded, by the power of love. I realize that such a question ominously echoes the hypocritical cant of those who never tire of telling us that love can save the world, vanquish the forces of evil. Of course, those who preach this message quite frequently embody the very evil their message is secretly intended not to defeat but to protect. And yet, if we think about love seriously, by which I mean if we seriously take love to be a narcissistic extravagance, then we will acknowledge that, first of all, simply willing ourselves to cherish the differences of others will, in all likelihood, leave our murderous antagonism toward difference intact, and, secondly, that the myth of love can become its truth only if we reinvent the relational possibilities of narcissism itself. There is no solution easily recognizable as "political" to the political horrors evoked earlier in this discussion because no recognizably political solution can be durable without something approaching a mutation in our most intimate relational system. Foucault's call for "new relational modes" struck some of his readers as politically evasive; it seems to me, on the contrary, that his summoning us to rethink relationality is at once an instance of political realism and a moral imperative. A new challenge would be to imagine enlisting the ego in modeling an impersonal relational field. Might the ego also be an agent of impersonal narcissism?

Socrates doesn't like being in the country. Although he gives an appreciative and lovely description of the "beautiful resting place"—on a grassy slope under a plane tree near a spring running with very cool water and echoing "with the summery sweet song of the cicadas' chorus"—where he and his young friend Phaedrus (in the dialogue *Phaedrus)* decide to stop at the end of a walk outside the city walls, the principal appeal of the spot he chooses clearly has less to do with its beauty than with its suitability as a place for talk. "Landscapes and trees," Socrates declares, "have nothing to teach me; only people in the city can do that." So, far from sitting down to admire their chosen resting place in silence, Socrates, having given the rural retreat one good look, promptly ignores it in order to give himself over entirely to speech. Or, more exactly, to speeches: first, to listening to Phaedrus read a speech given in Athens by the orator Lysias, then to giving two speeches himself in response, and, much later in the dialogue, to an exchange with Phaedrus on the art of composing speeches and the relation between rhetoric and philosophy. In demonstrating, against Lysias, that it's better for a boy to give his favors to a man who loves him than to a nonlover, Socrates is led to praise the madness that, for Lysias, makes the self-controlled nonlover a safer choice and therefore preferable to the frenzied lover. (Socrates has made his task more difficult by using his first speech to criticize the lover more persuasively than Lysias did, sharpening the latter's recital of the dangers for the boy in giving himself to a jealous, irritable, deceitful mad lover.) Socrates must prove that the lover's madness "is given to us by the gods to ensure our greatest good fortune." That entails, logically, a defense of love itself, an argument that will precisely define the "good fortune" brought to us by love. Put in other, more characteristically Socratic terms, the philosopher must show that love nourishes the soul, fills it with beauty, goodness, and images of wisdom.

All soul is immortal. As the source of all movement in everything that moves, the soul itself has no beginning and cannot be destroyed. Unable to describe the soul "as it actually is," Socrates likens it "to the natural union of a team of winged horses and their charioteer." Souls patrol the heavens, following the gods as the latter make the steep climb to the high tier at the rim of heaven, where the (non-god) souls just barely have a view of the Reality "beyond heaven," the "being that really is what it is" that only the gods can view and know completely. Every soul follows a particular god in its heavenly flights; if its wings are no longer in perfect condition, it merely wanders "until it lights on something solid, where it settles and takes on an earthly body." Every human soul remains in touch, through memory, with the god it followed; it is, Socrates affirms, "inspired by [that god] and adopts his customs and practices, as far as a human being can share a god's life."

This, however, is not done in solitude; every embodied soul is surrounded by other embodied souls with similar histories. What, then, could be more natural than the reaction of those whose memory is "good enough" when they see "an image of what they saw up there"? They are "startled," "beside themselves"; they shudder, they are afflicted with a chill that "gives way to sweating and a high fever." Unable to see wisdom directly, vision, the sharpest of our senses, responds to human beauty as a reminder of heavenly Beauty. "A godlike face or bodily form that has captured" that Beauty drives us mad with pain and joy, with anguish and helpless raving; we can't sleep by night or stay put by day; we rush, yearning, to wherever we expect to see the person who has that beauty—in Socrates' account, this is of course a beautiful boy—and once we are in his presence the previously blocked sluice-gates of desire are opened, we forget mother, brother, friends, wealth, "proper and decorous behavior," all in order just to be near the object of our longing. "This," Socrates instructs Phaedrus, "is the experience we humans call love."

"The finding of an object is in fact a re-finding of it." Of course, the child sucking at its mother's breast, or the Lacanian *objet petit a* (the cause as distinct from the object of desire), which may be nothing more than fantasmatic feces, represents a considerable comedown, in the history of the human imagination of love, from Plato's "ultimate vision" of the beautiful, the true and the good. No matter; what does matter for us is the profound continuity, despite the great difference, between the modern and ancient concepts of love. In both cases, love is a phenomenon of memory, and an instance of narcissistic fascination. Love in Plato, as both *The Symposium* and *Phaedrus* make clear, is selflove, a relation of the subject to himself. But it is a form of narcissism that the psychoanalytical version of narcissism, which it appears to resemble, makes it difficult for us to understand. We should first of all note that there are, in *Phaedrus* as well as in *The Symposium,* two different concepts of love. The first, which is Platonic in inspiration, is a love consisting of the contemplation of pure Forms, a vision that, in its fullness, is reserved for the gods and in which we, as souls not yet weighted down by bodies, imperfectly participated. But once a soul is in a body, and depends on other bodies for images of those pure Forms, its relation to the remembered Forms themselves significantly changes. It's true that "a few people [presumably philosophers] are able to make out, with difficulty, the original of the likenesses they encounter here," but even they appear to depend on the likenesses for their access to the original. If this were not the case, Socrates might enjoy the country more than he does; he could find many resting places like the one that provides the setting for his dialogue with Phaedrus, and he would of course have no need of Phaedrus in order to contemplate, rapturously, those "sacred, revealed objects"—whose essences owe nothing to the being of Socrates the man—"objects that were perfect, and simple, and unshakable and blissful." Even Socrates—especially Socrates, according to the jealous Alcibiades of *The Symposium* —needs to be in the company of beautiful boys; the city's meeting places are the sites of a metaphysical sociability sympathetic to the beneficent madness of love.

The Platonic contemplation of ideal Forms is transformed by that sociability. The boy we madly love does not simply remind us of the Beauty we saw before being imprisoned in a body. Remember that every soul followed a particular god in his heavenly flights; on earth, "every one spends his life honoring the god in whose chorus he danced." This entails seeking a boy "whose nature is like the god's": "those who followed Zeus, for example," as Socrates explains, "choose someone to love who is a Zeus himself in the nobility of his soul.... Hera's followers look for a kingly character"; and the same is true for former followers of Apollo or any other god. In other words, we seek, through love, not only to relive, albeit imperfectly, the "ultimate vision" of absolute ideas some of us may have shared with the gods; we also wish to revive the memory of the god in whose company we pursued that vision. The boy's beauty is a likeness of ideal Beauty; more specifically, he also has a particular nature that is like the type of being most fully realized in a particular god.

The soul that pursues "that which really is what it is" is, then, not pure lack, an empty desiring receptacle; it has a recognizable moral character. It is individualized not in the way that personalities are, to our modern psychological understanding, individualized. Rather, it has what might be thought of as a general, universal, individuation. The lover seeks to make the lover like himself, but this has nothing to do with the specularity of a personal narcissism. He chooses a boy who already belongs to the lover's type of being; and then, as Socrates puts it, he pours into the boy's soul more of the particular god's "inspiration" that made the lover choose him in the first place. That is, in making "every possible effort to draw [the boy they love] into being totally like themselves and the god to whom they are devoted," lovers are at the same time attempting to make the boy *more like himself.* The lover narcissistically loves the image of his own universal individuation that he implants in the boy he loves, but he is implanting more of what his beloved is, more of the type of being they already share. Far from suppressing the other, the Socratic lover's narcissism suppresses accidents of personality so that the loved one may more adequately mirror the universal singularity mythified in the figure of the god they both served.

This extraordinary anatomy of love leads to what Foucault celebrated, and others have recognized, as an anomaly in Greek love: erotic reciprocity. The beloved becomes a lover as a result of being loved.

How? Just as lovers are, according to Socrates, "startled" when they see an image of what they had glimpsed in heaven, so the boy begins by being "amazed at the exceptional friendship the lover offers him." The boy's beauty makes desire flow so abundantly in the lover that "it overflows and runs away outside him." "Think," Socrates explains, "how a breeze or an echo bounces back from a smooth solid object to its source; that is how the stream of beauty goes back to the beautiful boy and sets him aflutter." It enters his soul through his eyes; "there it waters the passages for the wings, starts the wings growing, and fills the soul of the loved one in return. Then the boy is in love, but he has no idea of what he loves." It is as if he were stricken with a disease whose cause he can't identify. Socrates explicitly identifies the narcissistic nature of this love: the boy "does not realize he is seeing himself in the lover as in a mirror, and now he will yearn for the lover as much as the lover yearns for him, "because he has a mirror image of love in him." (This type of love, anteros in Greek, has been translated as "counterlove" and as "backlove.") The beloved loves the lover's image of him, which is of course the version of himself that makes the lover remember both heavenly Beauty and the god with whom the lover's soul had flown. The boy loves a soul that he both is and is becoming, the latter as a result of the lover's pouring more and more into him the qualities of the god whose nature the lover had already seen in the boy. In Freudian terms, we might say that the boy sees and loves his ideal ego in his lover—except that this ego is not exactly something that he has lost and that he projects onto some one else, the over-valued object of love. On the contrary: it is what the lover loves in him. In a sense, the lover recognizes *his* ideal ego in the boy; desiring the boy is a way of infusing the boy with an ideal self that is both the boy's and the lover's. The lover's desire waters the smaller, less developed wings of a soul very much like his. And as the wings of the beloved's ideal nature grow, the lover is transported—driven divinely mad—by his vision of the boy becoming more and more like himself (the boy), like him (the lover), and like the god they both serve, the type of being to which they both belong."

The miracle in all this is that when we describe this love as narcissistic, we must also say that it is pure object-love. In a recent essay entitled "Desiring by Myself," Adam Phillips makes the following "clinical proposition": "Our wishes are unmarried to the world." Commenting on Jacques-Alain Miller's notion of "extimacy," Phillips defines the analytic project as learning "to bear being possessed" by a "desiring source" that is at once within the subject and "other" than the subject. "Desire, in this picture," Phillips writes, "is like being told a secret about oneself that some one else has made up." The *Phaedrus* at once confirms and proposes an alternative to this account. What both the beloved and the lover love are "secrets" about themselves *and* the truth about the other. The lover's desire is not that which he fails to recognize as his; rather, it is the reality of the other that he remembers and embraces as his own. Backlove is self-love, but the self the boy sees and loves in the lover is also the lover's self, just as the lover, in remembering and worshipping his own godlike nature in the boy, is also worshipping the boy's real (ideal) soul. Narcissistic love in both the lover and the beloved (can they even still be distinguished?) is exactly identical to a perfect knowledge of otherness.

I call this love impersonal narcissism because the self the subject sees reflected in the other is not the unique personality central to modern notions of individualism. National, ethnic, and racial identities are like personal egos in that they can be defined as historically distinct and inherently oppositional identities. Christianity and homosexuality, to take two examples of collective identity, are in reality anything but monolithic identitarian blocks. And yet, despite their diffused presence throughout the world, as well as their diverse modes of expression, the imaginary spaces in which they are enclosed create equally imaginary yet powerfully operative borders outside of which lies everything that is essentially different from them. Individual and collective egos must always be ready to defend those borders, and because such egos are by nature settled or congealed differences, they are inclined to define themselves, indeed to construct the unity of their being, in terms of an aggressively defensive posture toward the differences outside their identitiarian frontiers. The hyperbolizing of the ego I discussed earlier is a self-identifying exercise in which the ego can experience itself as a militant identity. Ancient Greek culture was apparently just as versatile as ours in framing being within oppositional identities: citizen-slave, male-female, active-passive, the lover and the beloved (*erastes* and *eromenos)*. Remarkably, Plato's *Phaedrus* breaks out of this field of knowability. Specifically, it undoes the opposition between the active lover and the passive loved one by instituting a kind of reciprocal self-recognition in which the very opposition between sameness and difference becomes irrelevant as a structuring category of being.

What Socrates describes as something we remember can be reformulated as the psychic anteriority of our *virtual being* in relation to the quotidian manifestations of our individual egos. Virtual being is unmappable as a distinct identity; it *is* only in becoming more like itself. In the generous narcissism of the exchange between Socratic lovers, each partner demands of the other (as we see Socrates demanding of Alcibiades in the dialogue *Alcibiades)* that he reflect the lover's type of being, his universal singularity (and not his psychological particularities, his personal difference), by recognizing and cultivating that singularity as his own most pervasive, most pressing potentiality. If we were able to relate to others according to this model of impersonal narcissism, what is different about others (their psychological individuality) could be thought of as merely the envelope of the more profound (if less fully realized, or completed) part of themselves which is our sameness. Naturally, each subject's type of being is not reflected in everyone else. But the experience of belonging to a family of singularity without national, ethnic, racial, or gendered borders might make us sensitive to the ontological status of difference itself as what I called the nonthreatening supplement of sameness in *Homos.*

The relationality I have just sketched could amount to a revolutionary reversal of the relational mode dominant in our culture, one that nourishes the powers of evil that govern us and with which, as long as we remain in this relational field, we are all complicit. In Socrates' version of love, the wings on which we can soar to our virtual ideal being need constantly to be watered. Unlike the more specifically Platonic world of ideas—immobile and unchanging in "the place beyond heaven"—Socratic ideality (which I am equating with universal virtualities) is more cultivated than it is contemplated. Cultivated through dialogue—intrinsically unending dialogue, for we are always either moving toward or falling away from the being it is our greatest happiness to "re-find" in others. Small wonder that Socrates is reluctant to venture far from the meeting places of the city. Like all of us, he needs talk, not only with the liberal aim of exchanging and testing ideas, but to exercise what he alludes to as our distinctive human capacity to use and to understand language as our only guide to the virtual being that continuously becomes, through speech, more like itself. The ascetic ethic Foucault was drawn to in antiquity was perhaps most expertly practiced by Socrates who, much to the exasperation of Alcibiades in his role as sexual seducer, identified a life devoted to love as a lifelong devotion to philosophical discussions—or, to put it not quite so dryly, to spiritually liquefying speech.

FOUR

On a More Impersonal Note

The preoccupation with so-called boundary-violations in contemporary psychoanalysis—the sometimes forlorn attempts to regulate psychoanalytic practice to ensure that patients are not exploited by their therapists—betrays an anxiety that the psychoanalytic setting can be rather more like ordinary life than psycho analysts want it to be. Whenever there is a boundary-violation, whenever the analyst behaves inappropriately in the treatment, it is as if, to put it at its most abstract, the analyst has been guilty of a category error. He has started treating the analytic situation as though it were not a place apart, but as though it were a place, like many others, in which one might find a friend or even a lover. The psycho-analyst is the one who is supposed to know the difference—both in himself and in his patient—between transference love and the other kind. Some people, it is assumed, can be less unconscious of the provenance and nature of their desire. So when Lacan remarked that the well-analyzed analyst is more rather than less likely to fall in love with his patient he was reminding us—as Freud had done in his great and confounded essay of 1915, "Observation on Love in Transference"—that we are at our most insistent about boundaries when we sense their precariousness.

Transference love, as Freud says, "consists of reissuing old components and repeating infantile reactions. But that is always the essence of falling in love." The well-analyzed analyst, in Lacan's terms, is more the subject of his own desire—or more subject to his desire—and his desire is by (Freudian) definition forbidden, endangering. From a psychoanalytic point of view, as Bersani suggests, love is always the problem, and only apparently the solution. And whatever else it is, it is always a boundary-violation.

Approached developmentally from an objectrelations point of view in which, to use Ronald Fairbairn's emblematic tag "Libido is not pleasure-seeking but object-seeking," one might say something like, the mother loves the baby before the baby loves the mother. No baby has ever loved his mother, but he has wanted her, needed her, and in a certain sense desired her. Love as an artefact of the ego, love as something the child will eventually hear of as something much spoken about comes late in the day. But what comes really quite early in the day—well before love as the great legitimator, as the great stylist of desire—according to the psychoanalytic story is the differentiation, or otherwise of what we call, as observers, the subject and the object. And what is always most striking—what is always described despite the difficulty of giving an account—is the violence entailed in the move from narcissism toward a so-called object. Indeed the paradox that object-relations theory presents us with is that the individual's narcissism is seen as the saboteur of his development, development (maturity) in this picture involving exchange with real objects recognized as beyond omnipotent control. And yet what is taken to mobilize the greatest violence in the individual is the abrogation of his narcissism. The very thing one needs to do, the very thing one's development apparently requires is the very thing that unleashes the most violent destructiveness. There is, one might say, a tragic flaw in this absurdly self-defeating story. In promoting the developmental necessity of overcoming narcissism, object-relations theorists have been, as it were, encouraging the greatest possible violence between people. It is presumably not incidental that the theory most committed to the malignity of narcissism, to the acknowledgment of difference between the subject and his objects is also the psychoanalytic story renowned for its obsession with the death drive and its devotion to the individual's sadism. The most cursory reading of Melanie Klein and her followers ratifies Bersani's contention that in talking against narcissism—or in misreading it—psychoanalysts have created the problem they have been trying to solve. If the greatness of psychoanalysis, for Bersani, is "its attempt to account for our inability to love ourselves and others," then the future of psychoanalysis, if it is not to be yet another modern form of domesticity, if it is to have something unusual to add, must involve a radical redescription of love that is at once illuminating and clinically useful. And it may involve, as Ferenczi hoped

94

and as Bersani suggests at the beginning of this book, using the analytic relation—what Lacan called more fetchingly the psychoanalytic opportunity—as a vital clue to new forms of loving outside the analytic situation. To Bersani's implicit question in this book, why is self-destructiveness equated with self-hatred? we have to add the complementary question, why is self-love equated with hatred of reality? The analytic situation as Freud constructed it, in its extreme intimacy and extreme impersonality—though never quite as extreme as many of its devotees want it to be, which is itself telling—was just the place for these questions. The psychoanalyst becomes intimate with someone by not taking what they say personally. The patient acknowledges the most intimately anonymous part of himself, his desire, through not, as we say, getting to know the analyst. What kind of love is this? Or, to put it more transitively, to give it an object, what could this be a love of, or a love for? To answer this question, or to see if it is answerable, we need to look at Bersani's abiding preoccupation with the self-shattering of the ego. It is through the self-shattering of the ego—and of this being, in a sense, the desire of the ego—that "impersonal narcissism" begins to make its own unsensible sense.

If the ego's project is plausibility—satisfyingly coherent narrative accounts of the subject's wants and moves it is only through sexuality, in the Freudian account, that the ego can disturb itself. The sexual becomes, as it were, the individual's self-cure for his own plausibility, the sexual identified as that which irremediably violates the individual's intelligibility (to himself and others). As a clinical practice, psychoanalysis is committed to the unsettling of the individual's hardwon (i.e., defensive) self-knowledge; so-called self-knowledge, in this stark reversal of traditional priorities, becomes the obstacle rather than the instrument of the individual's satisfaction. Pleasure and pain, contrary to the ethos of utilitarian calculation, undo the calculating machine. In Bersani's reading of Freud—and this has been his abiding preoccupation—pain and pleasure, blurred by the sexual, become the means to a quite different sense of an end. "Pleasure and pain," he writes in *Baudelaire and Freud,* continue to be different sensations (in Freud's *Three Essays on the Theory of Sexuality)* "but, to a certain extent, they are both experienced as sexual pleasure when they are strong enough to shatter a certain stability or equilibrium of the self ... Sexuality would be that which is intolerable to the structured self." That which, from its own point of view apparently seeks its own satisfaction seeks, by the same token, its own ablation. Shattering, with its connotation of shock and fragmentation—and the implication that that which is shattered can never be repaired—has been Bersani's word for the ego's darker design in which the satisfaction more truly sought is a fortifying dissolution not a monumental achievement. And it is a talent for masochism—or to put it in the language of object-relations, which object-relations theorists would not be keen to do, masochism as a developmental achievement—that for Bersani through Freud, is the way to go.

What masochism makes possible is the pleasure in pain; or rather what masochism reveals is the capacity to bear, the capacity to desire the ultimately overwhelming intensities of feeling that we are subject to. In this sense the masochistic is the sexual, the only way we can sustain the intensity, the restlessness, the ranging of desire. Freud, like Lacan, is struck by how difficult it is for the modern individual to maintain his appetite for appetite; that the acquisition of (modern) identity involves the sacrificing of desire, and identity without desire is a futile passion. The individual tries to, in both senses, fix himself in a definably boundaried and accountable self, while the desire that animates him lives by mobility. "The masochistic excitement," Bersani and Ulysse Dutoit write in *The Forms of Violence,* "which perhaps initiates us to sexuality can therefore be exploited not as the goal of representation, but rather as a psychic 'technique' for destabilizing representations and maintaining mobility." Knowing what one wants is an incitement to violence. Selfhood—the self constituted through prior and assured knowledge of what it desires, that is, stable representations—can only be constructed by the repudiating, by the censoring and punishing and trivializing of desire. This is why, as Bersani famously remarked in his 1987 essay "Is the Rectum a Grave?" "There is a big secret about sex:

most people don't like it." If selfhood is your object of desire, sexuality will by defintion become a persecution; it will make a mockery where there should have been a satisfaction. It is strange how unwilling we are to acknowledge that such loyalties, such relishing of the death-in-life can only unleash, can only provoke the most lethal violence.

There is, perhaps paradoxically, a struggle that Bersani wants us to resist, the struggle for what he calls selfhood. So there is selfhood or *jouissance:* the (sadistic) ego with its developmental achievements, its masterful plausibility, or the self-shattering (masochistic) ego that Bersani wants to make the case for without falling into what Wilde called "careless habits of accuracy." Without, that is to say, replacing one form of mastery with another, without the prescriptions for a new normativity. The ways in which we are invited to "resist projects of subjection" are likely to subject us to something. So I want to quote at length from the extraordinary final paragraph of "Is the Rectum a Grave?" because I think of it now as a kind of prelude or foretaste—a warning against, and a provocation toward—the "impersonal narcissism," the new power of love that Bersani is proposing in this book. "Whatever is turned away from," Joseph H. Smith writes, "is marked as a danger to be faced or a loss to be mourned." I want to consider, in the psychoanalytic way, what are the dangers to be faced and the losses to be mourned, or more cheerfully ignored, in Bersani's proposition. The "murderous judgement" against the gay man, Bersani writes, is grounded in the sacrosanct value of selfhood, a value that accounts for human beings' extraordinary willingness to kill in order to protect the seriousness of their statements. The self is a practical convenience; promoted to the status of an ethical ideal, it is a sanction for violence. If sexuality is socially dysfunctional in that it brings people together only to plunge them into a self-shattering and solipsistic jouissance that drives them apart, it could also be thought of as our primary hygienic practice of non-violence. Gay men's "obsession" with sex, far from being denied, should be celebrated ... because it never stops re-presenting the internalized phallic male as an infinitely loved object of sacrifice. Male homosexuality advertises the risk of the sexual itself as the risk of self-dismissal, of losing sight of the self, and in so doing it proposes and dangerously represents jouissance as a model of ascesis.

The losses to be mourned, ironic as some of them may be, are not, I suspect, as daunting as the fears to be faced. There is the loss of the sacrosanct value of selfhood—a refuge, as the phrasing suggests, for the sacred and its attendant pieties—and the loss of both a willingness to kill, and the seriousness of statements. There is the loss of the (domestic) fantasy of sexuality enshrining family values, the loss of Kant's categorical imperative, the loss, in short, of a story about sexuality that is in fact a story about the sacrificing of sexuality. We have to imagine a "social" world, as Bersani intimates in this book, in which the fundamental question, the abiding concern is, "do you want to have sex with me?" everything following from the answer. Once the sexual is staged as the losing sight of self rather than its assertion or consolidation or indeed triumph, the obsession with sex becomes an obsession with a certain kind of love. Bersani, I think, is wanting to imagine forms of desire that are not forms of revenge. The primary loss to be mourned is for the violence necessitated by the protection of selfhood (Bersani's answer to Auden's question "Is a shield a weapon?" would be yes). We would have to learn to stop taking sex personally.

The fears to be faced, of course, are inextricable from the losses to be mourned. The fear of *jouissance,* despite and because of the longing for it—not to mention the dread of "modes of ascesis"—is not to be underestimated. Selfhood wasn't built in a day; and defenses, developmentally, are the order of the day. Bersani's description of sex here, of how it might be thought of as "our primary hygienic practice of nonviolence," might make one wonder what the fear of nonviolence might be, what we would be giving up and having to face in the giving up of a certain kind of violence? It is unfortunate that the word "surrender" has connotations of defeat as well as of relief, but fortunate that yielding is also something we do to temptation. Against the violent and domineering assertions of selfhood—we can take the child's tantrum as an emblem for this, the demonic violence mobilized to protect, to hold out for the apparently known want—we have little to offer by way of description. If the ego's project, as Bersani says in this book, is "a defensive move (or a pre-emptively offensive move) against the world's threatening difference from the self" and there is, as Freud says in *Civilization and its Discontents,* "an extraordinarily high degree of narcissistic enjoyment" in satisfied aggression, then what could wean the ego from such satisfactions, what could possibly compete with the allure of these horrifying fundamental pleasures? What Bersani seems to suggest is that we tend not to be sufficiently narcissistic: that, to use an old language, we don't quite have the courage of our narcissism. It is not that we need to inhibit our narcissism, it is that our narcissism is itself inhibited. We are at our most controlled (and controlling) in our regulation of narcissistic desire.

Bersani's redescription of love, in other words, involves a redescription, a refinement of our assumptions about narcissism. "What is uniquely psychoanalytic," Bersani writes, "is the notion that the pleasurable power of satisfied aggression is itself a threat to the agent of aggression. In Freudian terms, the hyperbolic ego risks being shattered by its own narcissistically thrilling inflation." There is, in this picture, a paradoxical project; in the ego's necessary project of abolishing difference the ego runs the risk of abolishing itself (what Bersani calls "a cultivation of the superior power of the ego's suicidal self-love over its self-preservative aptitude for critical evaluation.") The ego's narcissistic forms of psychic self-preservation *are* the ways it destroys itself. To have the courage of one's narcissism—to find a version of narcissism that is preservative at once of survival and pleasure—would be to have the courage of one's wish for more life rather than less. The ego's revenge on the world for its difference, for its resistance, could be replaced by ... what? "Why is difference always linked with hatred?" Coleridge wrote somewhere in his notebooks. An obsession with difference is an obsession with hatred. What Bersani calls "willing ourselves to cherish the difference of others" may not be a commitment to others—to the so-called otherness of others, to other people as so-called ends in themselves—but a commitment to our own hatred. Love is nothing personal, difference always is.

The ego, as conceived by Freud, wants to be personable, and to make everything personal. Where id was there ego shall be means whatever is strange about myself I must make familiar, recognition must replace bewilderment. Encouraged to love the very difference that we are driven to abolish is the double bind of our modern sentimental education, a bind re-inforced by certain versions of psychoanalysis. It seems improbable, at first sight, that the ego could be recruited to be what Bersani calls "an agent of impersonal narcissism," a fashioner or sponsor of the relational possibilities of narcissism. Psychoanalysis may have relieved us of the ridiculous demand to love

others for themselves, and at the same time demand-
ed that we do nothing less. What Bersani wants to
keep open is the question of what we might love
others for, what in others we might love that would
curb the violence in our human-all-toohuman personal
relations.

Freud outlined the problem, without recourse to
the concept of narcissism, in his great paper of 1925,
"Negation." It is Freud's story of the construction of
what we might call identity, and Bersani calls selfhood,
though Freud of course does not use either term. The
ego constitutes itself through discrimination, it makes
itself up in the making of value judgements, and one
set of value judgments is above all formative. In this
picture the ego, by definition, could never be beyond
good and evil. The ego, analogous in Freud's strange
mixture to a court of law, an empirical scientist and
an aesthete, makes judgements:

Essentially it is the function of judgment to make
two kinds of decision. It has to decide whether or not
a thing possesses a certain property, and whether or
not an imagined thing exists in reality. The property
to be decided on might originally have been good or
bad, useful or harmful, or, expressed in the language
of the most archaic oral drive impulses: "I want to
eat this or spit it out." In more general terms: "I want
to take this into me, or keep it out of me," that is:
"I want it inside me, or outside me." As I have explained elsewhere, the primal pleasure-ego wants to
introject into itself everything good and expel from

itself everything bad. That which is bad, that which is alien to the ego, that which is outside, are initially identical as far as it is concerned.

Freud, it should be noted, is not saying in this passage from "The Unconscious" that that which is bad, that which is alien to the ego, that which is outside has to be destroyed; he is saying that it just has to be placed and kept outside. The other implication is that anything that is good will be experienced as though it was already inside; the puzzle might be something like, do I love it because it is inside me, or is it inside me because I love it? The word "love" is also not used here or in the paper, which is itself perhaps of interest, because one of the things that Freud would seem to be talking about here is the origin of love (the original version of the question do you want to have sex with me? would be the question do I want to eat you or spit you out?). For something (or someone) to be loveable it must be already inside one, or we must want it to be inside. In terms of survival the question becomes how to keep the unloved thing out. A world with nothing bad in it would have no outside (and in that sense, therefore, no inside either); the violence here is in the forms of rejection, of expulsion, and, presumably, in the policing of the borders. But perhaps the most striking thing about this primary project, this character-building scene, is that there can be no confusion, no ambiguity, no uncertainty about the status of what is to be taken in and what expelled. It is as though the ego already knows its own mind. Nothing can be un-recognizable, nothing can be paradoxical, nothing can be a mixed bag, nothing can be both inside and out-side. This is the narcissism of major differences. Things and people are loved, that is, taken and kept in; they can only be loved because they are not other, that is, outside and alien. To love what is other is to love what cannot be loved; it is like being force fed, and like being force fed it could only unleash an ex-treme violence, or the extreme stifling of violent en-ergies called depression. To be encouraged, to be educated, to be forced to drink what you would by desire spit out, is a form of torture. This is our pre-ferred model of love relations, this loving of the other for their difference. It is a picture we cannot afford not to do without. What Bersani proposes as a coun-termeasure—as an antiredemptive myth of sexual re-lations, in which neither the subject nor the object can be redeemed by love, but can only be lost—brings with it an instructive range of difficulties, the difficul-ties suggested, though, making it all the more remark-able.

Love as recovery—love as restoration of the earlier self, the early mother—is bound to be a furious project; as though sexual development was about waiting for an opportunity to get everything back that one had lost in the process of development. And in the full knowledge, as it were, that such restitution is impossible; hoping for the past, hoping for the supposedly already known, the supposedly already experienced is itself a form of despair, a horror of the new. Against the modernist injunction to "make it new," the modern Freudian subject, at least in his erotic life, keeps making it old, keeps rendering his own unknown future, his unknowable potential for loving, apparently familiar. Indeed, Freud seems to suggest that the modern individual's response to the new is to fall in love, as a self-cure (see my *Waiting for Returns* for an elaboration of this point). What Bersani calls here the "narcissistic extravagance" of love, its militant nostalgia, is an attempt to abolish the possibility of new experience. What we call love is our hatred of the future; and it is because other people represent our future as objects of desire, what might happen next to us, we fear them. It is this that makes the ego the most confounding object in the Freudian triumvirate. The ego, for its very survival, has to seek out new (i.e., "other") objects that it cannot bear because they are new; and it is prohibited by the incest taboo from seeking out the old objects that it desires, and cannot bear because they are forbidden. What the (Freudian) subject wants he must not have, and what he can have he will never quite want. If the ego's project is (psychic) survival, rage is going to be the order of the day.

In this sense the ego is a split subject, let alone the subject itself. Self-preservation and what Bersani calls "suicidal self-love," the "ultimately self-destructive will to master the world" are not merely incompatible. The ego's essential perplexity was Freud's way of saying that the modern individual could have more existence only by having less life (or "aliveness," to use Donald Winnicott's word). Modern love was a self-consuming passion. And yet, as Bersani points out, all of this comes out of sameness and difference as the constitutive terms of our being. We need—though this would not, I think, be Bersani's way of putting it—a new vocabulary, new ways of putting what can go on between people that do not presume a lethal antagonism. What is interesting about Bersani's description of impersonal narcissism is how it links with a language that is at once germane though rarely explicitly alluded to in Bersani's work: the language of early development, of mothers and fathers and babies. What, after all, is more central to post-Freudian accounts of early mothering than the notion of what Bersani calls "reciprocal self-recognition in which the very opposition between sameness and difference becomes irrelevant as a structuring category of being"? The impersonality of mothering, one might say, is the precursor, the precondition of an impersonal narcissism.

But if mothering could be described, however counterintuitively, as a profoundly impersonal intimacy, it is fathering, the developmental myth will tell us, that personalizes things. It is triangulation, contemporary psychoanalytic theory insists, that is the forcing house of self-conscious singularity. There are, the story tells us, two constitutive breaches in the infant's omnipotent narcissism: the dawning recognition that the needed mother is beyond omnipotent control, and the dawning acknowledgment that the mother desires (and is desired by) someone (or something) other than the infant. Sameness, in the old language, is violated by difference: where I was, there are now others. Other people, whatever they are, are the source of my frustration. My desire may be in excess of any object's capacity to satisfy it, but I am not going to begin by believing this. In this common-sense object-relations story, rage and its concomitants—sulking, resentment, withdrawal, the grudge and the generalized grievance—are the signs of difference registered. It is assumed though that the three-person relationship of the Oedipal triangle produces a person that can take things personally (it is as though, in this account, we have to imagine the baby, when noticing the mother independent of his need, thinks that something has gone wrong with his omnipotence, whereas in the Oedipal triangle he thinks that there is something the matter with him). In love so conceived there is the wish to get back before these catastrophes and the (enraged) sense of the impossibility of so doing. We live our lives forward but we desire backwards.

The Platonic account—which is not ostensibly an account of parenting at all, though to psychoanalytic ears it sounds like parenting at one remove, parenting with more of an option on impersonality—has, as Bersani makes clear, certain resemblances to the Freudian story about love. Just as Freud referred on several occasions to psychoanalytic treatment as an "aftereducation" (see, for example, *An Outline of Psychoanalysis),* the education of a psychoanalysis coming after the education in love that is parenting, so the Platonic education comes after the boy's parenting and before his manhood. The older man loves the boy, but is absolutely unlike a parent in that he is a lover in a way that the parent cannot be. One thing perhaps intimated in Bersani's use of the Platonic dialogues is that the lover can do something for the beloved (and vice versa) that the parent and child cannot do for each other; indeed that impersonal narcissism may require the after-education Plato describes, and that the family by definition cannot provide. The Socratic love relation, if it is not a displaced redescription of parenting, becomes a necessary reworking of what began in the family but could never be brought to fruition there; and not because of triangulation but because of the distraction of bisexuality. In other words, Bersani's linking, albeit through their differences, the psychoanalytic and the Platonic stories about love, raises two related questions; does his proposed version of impersonal narcissism require the after-education of a lover outside the family to be realized, and does the love relation need to be the same sex for such reciprocal self-recognitions to occur? These seem to me to be pertinent questions because virtually everything Bersani describes the Platonic lovers as doing for each other could be redescribed as something a mother or a father could to some extent do for their child, though not both together, not at the same time, as it were, and not necessarily—or not so easily, or not in the same way—with a child of the opposite sex. And were this to be a form of parenting it would be one in which, uniquely, differentiation—separation in the direction of increasing self-reliance or so-called independence—would be toward increasing supplements of what Bersani calls "nonthreatening sameness" (sameness becoming that which need not be attacked or destroyed).

Consider these lines from Bersani: "The beloved becomes a lover as a result of being loved" or "the boy's beauty makes desire flow so abundantly in the lover that it overflows and runs away outside him" or "the beloved loves the lover's image of him"; these are all the kinds of things that psychoanalytic theorists say about mothers and babies, but not, perhaps unsurprisingly, about fathers and babies. And by the same token the mother can be described as "attuned" above all, to the virtual being of her baby, his becoming of himself as he changes. What Bersani calls "virtual being" and might also be called "potential being" as long as the potential is always seen as an unknowable (i.e., unpredictable) category would be precisely the object of this kind of love; change would be conceived of as neither consolidation, renovation or, indeed development, but rather as innovation. When the new becomes the object of desire, the new has to be redescribed as more of the same. When narcissistic desire becomes the medium for recognition rather than the obstacle—as it does in mothering—it is affinity more than difference that is felt (it is when the baby is experienced by the mother as alien, as not of a piece with the mother, that something is radically wrong). Without in any way idealizing—or even referring to—the mother-infant relationship, Bersani's account of impersonal narcissism has elements, selected elements, of the primal scene of narcissism. Or at least seeing it in this way lets us ask what Bersani wants to take out of mothering—or parenting, in its familiar versions—that might make impersonal narcissism a viable possibility.

"If we were able to relate to others according to this model of impersonal narcissism," he writes, "what is different about others (their psychological individuality) could be thought of as merely the envelope of the more profound (if less fully realized or completed) part of themselves which is our sameness." An envelops both protects and makes transmission possible. If binaries are to be avoided we can't simply say that our differences are our best defense against our sameness, that so-called difference is merely a technique for distance-regulation, that sameness as our most longed for, if not forbidden pleasure is, by the same token, our greatest terror. We can say, though, that we use our putative differences, our cherished idiosyncracies to conceal from ourselves and others the affinities that always already exist. Bewitched by the armor of singularity, of a picture of individual identity that has to be fought for and fought over, the question for Bersani is, how can we allow our-selves—or, how can we remind ourselves—of our passion for sameness? How has the same become the forbidden, or less dramatically, the proscribed? As Bersani points out, in the *Phaedrus* the flourishing of the lover and his beloved through narcissistic mutual recognition, through the cultivation of sameness, is made possible by a background cosmology. The psy-choanalytic story, as a modern materialism, has more to say about desire and need, mothers and fathers, the unconscious, and the forbidden than about souls, heavenly flights, and gods followed. What then, from a psychoanalytic point of view, would make narcissistic desire the only accurate form of recognition, and the least violent?

Many years ago in supervision with the Kleinian analyst Donald Meltzer, I asked him whether he thought the analytic patient was capable in analysis of making truthful interpretations about the analyst, of seeing the analyst as he really is (in those days we could still speak like this). And he replied, without a moment's thought, "yes, absolutely, but only when the patient is at his most regressed in the transfer-ence." I was, then, very struck by this and asked him how it could be true. Equally surprisingly he replied, "When the patient is at his most regressed in the transference he is like a baby who can talk." Unlike the mother and the baby, of course, the Socratic lover and his beloved—not to mention the analyst and his analysand—talk to each other; and they are all involved, in their different ways, in getting to know each other through unconscious desire. There is, as Bersani remarks, no other guide than language "to the virtual being that continuously becomes, through speech, more like itself." We have to imagine that contradiction in terms the mothering of infants as linguistic exchange in which through the impersonal medium of language the mutual otherness of desire is played out. No amount of redescription will alter the fact that if people can satisfy each other they can frustrate each other. The impersonal narcissism of the psychoanalytic relation is, whatever else it is, a training in bearing frustration without resort to violence. If the quest for difference is a courting of frustration, and frustration is structurally ineradicable, we need to know what kinds of frustration the impersonal narcissist may be prone to, and why they won't make him violent.

If we start from the principle that a non- or anti-narcissistic love is no longer, indeed never was viable in terms of the violence it irremediably released, then we are free to consider what Bersani's impersonal narcissism would be freedom for and freedom from. What might we want from a new form of intimacy that the old forms protected us from? One of the many things that barebacking focuses for us—as both an emblem of impersonal intimacy, and of our fears of what it might involve—is, in the first instance at least, the relationship between shame and what might be called our freedom to describe the freedoms we might be capable of. In shame we are (violently) separated from our preferred image of ourselves—in psychoanalytic language we betray or sacrifice our ego-ideal—and so to bear with the experience of shame, to go through it rather than to be paralyzed by mortification, is to yield to a radical reconfiguration of oneself. The funneling scene in *Plantin' Seed* that Bersani describes in which Jonas is inseminated with the ejaculate of unknown men is the logical completion of intimate anonymity; "barriers of disgust and shame having been overcome," as Bersani remarks, acknowledging the sense in which the shame barrier may be integral to the experience. In so far as disgust and shame are the barriers to the impersonal they are, by the same token, the ways through.

Psychoanalysis, of course, has had things to say about guilt and shame which, in mainstream psychoanalysis, are more or less summed up by Joseph Sandler, Alex Holder, and Dale Meers in their paper "Ego-Ideal and Ideal Self." "Shame might be related to 'I cannot see myself as I want to see myself or as I want others to see me.' Guilt, on the other hand, would be associated with 'I do not really want to be what I feel I ought to be.'" In the experience of shame I fail to live up to the ideal standards I have accepted for myself (i.e., my egoideal), in guilt there is a disparity between my ideal-self and the self my parents (introjected as my super-ego) have dictated for me. So if to bear guilt is to free oneself, to some extent, from the obligations, the demands of (ultimately internalized) others, to bear shame is to free oneself of a complicity with others. Guilt, and particularly shame, however unconscious are fairly and squarely in the realm of the social, of the official and unofficial social contract. We are guilty when we contest and protest but when we are mortified we need to ask not merely what rule have we broken, but how impersonal can we be in our search for satisfaction? Shame, as I think barebacking exposes, is like a threshold from the personal to the impersonal, from consent to abandonment, from cherished and horrifying selfimages to those images of oneself that one could never have before the experience. It is a passage from obliteration of the known, itself a form of knowing, to the literally inconceivable. Guilt is what we feel about the forbidden, shame is what we feel on the verge of the unknown and unknowable. In this sense barebacking is not transgressive. It is, for want of a better, less camp word, pioneering. In other words it is going to make us horrifyingly intrigued, fascinated and morally confounded, but never indifferent.

In this picture shame confronts us with our inability, or unwillingness to be what we have consented to be. In this sense it is not, as in guilt, the undoing of something felt to be alien, but the undoing of something felt to be integral. We are coming apart from our preferred version of ourselves. It is a more radical dismantling of what has been assumed to be the most profoundly personal form of selfhood (what

I consent to, by so doing, I make essentially mine). "The root of shame," Bernard Williams writes, in a quite different context, "lies in exposure in a more general sense, in being at a disadvantage: in what I shall call, in a very general phrase, a loss of power. The sense of shame is a reaction of the subject to the consciousness of this loss: in Gabriele Taylor's phrase ... it is 'the emotion of self-protection.'" Where once there was the power of personal narcissism—the ego invested by and invested with personal commitments—there is now, as a preliminary to a more impersonal narcissism, the loss of power, a divestment. The moment of self-protection can be a moment of wondering whether the self is worth protecting; whether the cost of the agreed-to, agreed-upon selfhood is too great. The question is—and it is a question that can to some extent be addressed by so-called developmental theory—what has to happen to the consciousness of loss of power to make it a shameful experience rather than, say, a blissful one? Why, to ask an apparently daft question, would the self want to protect itself from the loss of power, from the consciousness of this loss? Loss of power, after all, might be the precondition for the longed for and feared experience of exchange, of intimacy, of desire indifferent to personal identity. When Christopher Bollas, for example, suggests in *The Shadow of the Object* that the mother of early infancy "is less significant and identifiable as an object than as a process that is identified with cumulative internal and external transformations," for mother we can read the one whose selfhood we need not recognize. Indeed it is our very powerlessness to do so at that stage that makes such cumulative transformations possible. The mother and infant may have a growing sense of what each other are like, but they are more attuned by their impersonal narcissistic investment in each other, to what each is becoming in the presence of the other. When the mother of infancy, as Hans Loewald writes in *Psychoanalysis and the History of the Individual,* "reflected 'more' to the child than he presented, when she, in her responsive activities was cognizant of his potential for future growth and development and mediated it to the infant," she is cognizant that he has potential, but not unless she is unduly omniscient of exactly what that potential might be. The mother usually knows what endangers the child, but not what he might become. The parents' wish to know the child, and the child's wish to know the parents (which is introjected from the parents)—the personalizing of their narcissistic investment in each other—is, at its most extreme, a defense against what is unknowably evolving, as potential, between them. This is a version, perhaps the originary one, of the desire for virtual being, what Bersani calls here, "the generous narcissism of the exchange between Socratic lovers." There is no relation more narcissistic, as Freud himself remarks, than the relation between mothers and their children; and there is, by the same token, no relation more devoted to or more inspired by the virtual, the potential. The first intimacy is an intimacy with a process of becoming, not with a person. The question raised by Bersani's account is why is this relation so difficult to sustain, so easily sabotaged by the drive to take things personally?

Barebacking, whatever else it is, is the attempt to recover, to recreate—but more realistically, in my view—something of this process of impersonal transformation. Its (secular) realism resides in its explicit acknowledgment that our idealization of growth and development—and what are so-called intimate relations in the service of now if not our putative personal development?—is an attempt to conceal from ourselves the fact that we are going nowhere: that we are growing toward extinction, children or no children. That the joke of evolution is that it is a teleology without a point, that we, like all animals, are a project that issues in nothing. Freud's notion of a death drive was, I think, one way of saying this: we want to die, and whether or not we want to we will. Barebacking shows us that sex is a dead end and it is our consciousness of this—what Bernard Williams refers to in *Shame and Necessity* as the consciousness of loss of power—that makes our human sexuality what it is. Reproductive sexuality shows us that in having children we are making more deaths; and it is this salient acknowledgment, conscious or not, that makes human sexuality possible. When Freud suggested, against Darwin, that the desire for pleasure might outstrip the desire to reproduce, and that the desire to die can be stronger than the desire for more life, that in every sexual act there are more than two people involved, that the object of desire was "soldered" on to the instinct and not integral to it, and that desire was always in excess of any object's capacity to satisfy it, he was, absurd as it might seem, exposing the impersonality of desire. If cruising reinstated this, barebacking takes it to its logical conclusion.

But we don't need the idea of a death drive, or even the rather less metaphysical notion of self-hatred to redescribe barebacking as something that we should not relish dismissing. Nor, I think, despite Bersani's misgivings, should we assume that it need not have to do with shame. In what he calls "the ascesis of an ego-divesting discipline," there may have to be a way through shame not a way round it. When Guillaume, as quoted by Bersani, makes the fascinating remark, "When no-one really exists there is room for every-one," we should see shame as the last gasp of someone really existing, of the ego as it begins to fall foul of itself, to outreach its own (representational) grasp. In shame the personal is beginning to give way, and the abjection, the mortification, the humiliation is a literal form of self-holding. One still has in these states a picture of who one should be, of what one should look like, even though the suffering is in this disparity, this unbridgeable gulf between who one feels oneself to be, and who one should be (suffering, as the psychoanalyst Joseph Sandler once remarked, in a rather abstract formulation, has to do with the distance between the ego and the ego-ideal). Shame, if anything, confronts one most vividly, that is, most terribly with the picture of who one wants to be through the experience of failing to be it. One is most essentially one's self at such moments. Not to be able to bear shame is not to be able to bear the possibility of not knowing who one might be. Shame is the sign of the approaching death of oneself as a recognizable person. The pursuit of shameful or shaming experiences is often the (unconscious and uncompleted) quest for ego-dissolution, for the erasure of the person as he wants to be. The most difficult thing about shame is to go through with it. This might require an ascetic self-discipline; barebacking may be one of the unofficial forms this ascesis has thus far taken. At their worst shame experiences consolidate the identity they are trying to dissolve. It may be truer, though more disturbing, to say that barebacking succeeds where shame too often fails. Shame flirts, albeit in the most painful way, with the dissolution of the ego; barebacking is more concerted, more intent. No one should in any way promote nonconsensual barebacking; but, perhaps by the same token, no one can afford to ignore what consensual barebacking presents us with—both as a reality and as cartoon—as a new form of and project for intimacy. Intimacy, perhaps above all as an openness to the ultimate in impersonality; it is the end of sex as our ultimately self-protective act. Barebacking faces a limit that reproductive sex never can. But because death is more impersonal than children we should not assume that barebacking is necessarily the worship—cynical or otherwise—of death. (It's not obvious why we assume that a longing for death is a hatred of life.) Barebackers clearly see a different kind of future in human relatedness. Barebacking is a picture of what it might be for human beings in relation with each other not to personalize the future. Impersonal intimacy asks of us what is the most inconceivable thing: to believe in the future without needing to personalize it. Without, as it were, seeing it in our own terms. To get back to the original question, but seeing it through the prism of barebacking, what is impersonal narcissism as a new form of intimacy freedom from and freedom for? How would our lives be better if human relations were something other than the collusion of ego-identities, if the shared project was not the consolidation of selfhood, but its dissolution? And how, rather more pressingly in the light of all-too recent and contemporary atrocities, could such a project be pursued as the mitigant rather than the cause of the most horrifying violence that we take to be of a piece now with our human nature? Is it possible, as Socrates says at the end of the *Phaedrus,* that "what is in my possession outside me may be in friendly accord with what is inside," and so not be possession at all?

CONCLUSION

One of the things that has always appealed to me in Adam Phillip's work is his use of anti-psychoanalytic arguments *for* psychoanalysis. For what I understand to be classical psychoanalytical theory, analysis is an investigation into a personal past. From this perspective, it could be thought of—indeed, has been thought of—as a depth psychology: the unconscious would add to our knowledge of the mind psychic contents never dreamt of by pre-Freudian psychology. Without denying the reality, and the therapeutic relevance, of such analytic staples as the stages of sexual maturation, the shapes and outcomes of the Oedipus complex, the interpretation of dreams, the analysis of symptoms, the classifications of neuroses and psychoses, the mechanisms of repression and sublimation, the illuminations and subterfuges of memory, the projection and introjection of good and bad objects, Phillips seems to be moving psychoanalytic theory and practice in other directions, directions already authorized, accord to him, by Freud himself. It is in the course of an introduction to Freud's writings on psychoanalytic technique that Phillips makes claims that my discussion of *Intimate Strangers* and *The Beast in the Jungle* was meant, in large part, to test, in particular the claim that the analytic dialogue might lead to the discovery that "there are other satisfactions than the satisfactions of personal history." I see this as a way of suggesting that the human subject can be more than a psychological subject, a suggestion reinforced by Phillips's view of Freud as "trying to describe, through the figure of the analyst, a new way of being present to another person," one that would free both the analyst and the patient "to think and speak freely." Analytic dialogue would thus depend less on the excavation of the secrets and conflicts in the analysand's past and more on a democratically conceived dialogue oriented toward an as yet undefined way of people "being present" to one another. Philosophically, this could be formulated as a prioritizing of being over knowledge—or, in other terms, a displacement from the search for psychic truth to an experience, and experiment, in relational transformations.

But why would we want to free ourselves from the personal? Selfhood—and the personal type of narcissism that appears to consolidate selfhood—is, as Phillips intimates, associated with power, and, as an important part of our argument, we have had to articulate both the appeal and the dangers of power (as well as the presumed danger of losing power). These are the issues I attempt to address in the section of this book on The Power of Evil and the Power of Love. My proposals involve a (highly speculative) unfolding of the logic that leads from the personal (from selfhood) to violence. As Freud asserts, the self seeks to appropriate a world perceived as hostile to its interests and even to its survival. Personal narcissism is an extreme form of appropriative possession: the world reduced to a specular image of the ego. Any such mastery of difference is of course an illusion, not only because, realistically, the world will always successfully resist projects that aim to erase its otherness, but also because the satisfaction given to the ego by that illusion is also destructive to the ego itself. The ego is shattered by the excitement of its illusory power; satisfied aggression is a threat to the agent of aggression (the hyperbolized ego). The impulse to destroy the world is inseparable from the *jouissance* of self-destruction.

In *The Freudian Body,* I spoke of masochism as an evolutionary conquest: it allows the infant to survive the gap between a period of shattering stimuli and the development of resistant, defensive ego structures. Loving to be shattered becomes a self-preservative strategy. There is obviously something deeply dysfunctional in this "solution" to the already biologically dysfunctional process of human maturation. The willfully inflated and shattered ego returns us to the masochistic intensities of the helplessly invaded infantile ego. If, to re-formulate one of Phillips's questions, we seek to protect ourselves from the loss of selfhood's (illusory) power, it may be because the violence "irredeemably released" by personal narcissism—violence toward the world and toward the self—is accompanied by a sexualized excitement with which, Freud claims in *Civilization and Its Discontents,* nothing else in life can compete. If it makes great sense to say that this is what we should want to protect ourselves *from,* it also seems to be true that, psychoanalytically considered, this is also what we seek to save ourselves—to (falsely) consolidate the self—*for.*

Our dialogue in this book could be thought of as an attempt to formulate alternatives to the violent games of selfhood. Phillips's version of the analytic exchange (an exchange at once imitated and repudiated by William and Anna in *Intimate Strangers),* the practice of barebacking and the cult of "pure love" it bizarrely resembles, and above all the Socratic definition of a love based on impersonal narcissism: all very different, yet all illustrative, in Phillips's words, of an "experience of exchange, of intimacy, of desire indifferent to personal identity." Although the satisfactions of these intimacies are not dependent on personal pasts, our emphasis on the future would be glibly utopic if it were not grounded in a re-imagining of the past. If "impersonal intimacy asks of us what is the most inconceivable thing: to believe in the future without needing to personalize it," the belief becomes at least somewhat conceivable if we can believe, to begin with, in an impersonal *past.* In the passage where he quotes from Christopher Bollas's fascinating discussion of "the transformational object," Phillips spells out developmental alternatives, within a person's past, to the personal. A psychoanalyst's interest in the past can, it turns out, be entirely compatible with an impersonal relationality. The mother of early infancy may be one "whose selfhood we need not recognize. Indeed, it is our very power-lessness to do so at that stage that makes [the] cumulative transformations [evoked by Bollas] possible." In *The Shadow of the Object,* Bollas describes a "being-with, as a form of dialogue," that enables "the baby's adequate processing of his existence prior to his ability to process it through thought." Phillips, elaborating on this wordless "dialogue," speaks of mother and infant being "attuned ... to what each is becoming in the presence of the other." (Bollas refers to the baby being transformed by the mother's "aesthetic of handling.") Phillips's formulation of course brings us back to the *Phaedrus;* it beautifully express-es the nature of the exchange between the Socratic lovers, an exchange in which, through a reciprocal attentiveness to the other's becoming what he potentially is, both partners move beyond what turns out to have been only a provisional distinction between the lover and the beloved. Could this sort of exchange make even the distinction between analyst and analysand a provisional, or perhaps a purely heuristic, one? In any case, it is not at all a question of elimi-nating memory from the analytic exchange, or from other impersonal investments. Love is perhaps al-ways—as both Plato and Freud suggest—a phe-nomenon of memory, but what is remembered in the expansive narcissism of an impersonal intimacy is not some truth about the self, but rather, as Phillips says, "a process of becoming," or, in other terms, evolving affinities of being.

The subject's wish to *know* the other, rather than being valued as our highest relational aspiration, should be seen, as Phillips writes of the relation between mother and child, as "a defense against what is unknowingly evolving, as potential," between them. The fundamental premise of impersonal narcissism is that to love the other's potential self is a form of selflove, a recognition that the partners in this intimacy already share a certain type of being (a sharing acknowledged by love). Can there be any doubt of how "our lives would be better" if they were guided by what might become a generalized recognition of our beingin-the-world (one not based on appetitive and destructive projections), rather than being ruled by a "collusion of ego-identities"? Phillips's final sentence is itself a more than adequate answer to the question he raises. Quoting Socrates wondering if "what is in my possession outside me may be in friendly accord with what is inside," he rightly concludes that this would "not be possession at all." The political consequences of any such "friendly accord" would be enormous, but it would be dishonest to claim that we know how, exactly, they might be effected. As I have said before, no immediately recognizable political solution to such atrocities as those I discuss in Chapter 3, while certainly desirable, would address the relational aberrations that make such atrocities perhaps not only possible but inevitable. To be cured of those aberrations requires a thorough re-appraisal of how we have been trained culturally to think of difference, and a necessarily ascetic resistance to the undeniable excitement of destructive and self-destructive violence. (Some concrete steps might be: a re-thinking—within, for example, the analytic exchange—of how we conduct dialogue; reorganizations of education and cultural institutions; training children never to see the world as "outside" the family, as something from which the family "protects" us.) It is indeed strange that we find it so difficult to welcome, as Phillips writes, the blissful nature of the loss of the power of selfhood—a power it was, in any case, always an illusion to think we possessed. Strange, and yet natural if we acknowledge, as I suppose we must, what may be the most profound "mistake" inherent in being human: that of preferring our opposition to the world we live in over our correspondence, our "friendly accord," with it.

Front Cover Flap

Two gifted and highly prolific intellectuals, Leo Bersani and Adam Phillips, here present a fascinating dialogue about the problems and possibilities of human intimacy. Their conversation takes as its point of departure psychoanalysis and its central importance to the modern imagination—though equally important is their shared sense that by misleading us about the importance of self-knowledge and the danger of narcissism, psychoanalysis has failed to realize its most exciting and innovative relational potential.

In pursuit of new forms of intimacy they take up a range of concerns across a variety of contexts. To test the hypothesis that the essence of the analytic exchange is intimate talk without sex, they compare Patrice Leconte's film about an accountant mistaken for a psychoanalyst, *Intimate Strangers,* with Henry James's classic novella *The Beast in the Jungle.* A discussion of the subculture of barebacking—gay men intentionally engaging in risky sex—delineates an intimacy that rejects the personal. Even serial killer Jeffrey Dahmer and the Bush administration's war on terror enter the scene as the conversation turns to the way aggression thrills and gratifies the ego. Finally, in a reading of Socrates' theory of love from Plato's *Phaedrus,* Bersani and Phillips call for a new form of intimacy which they term "impersonal narcissism": a divestiture of the ego and a recognition of one's non-psychological potential self in others. This revolutionary way of relating to the world, they contend, could lead to a new human freedom by mitigating the horrifying violence we blithely accept as part of human nature.

Charmingly persuasive and daringly provocative, *Intimacies* is a rare opportunity to listen in on two brilliant thinkers as they explore new ways of thinking about the human psyche.

Back Cover Flap

Leo Bersani is professor emeritus of French at the University of California, Berkeley. He is the author or coauthor of numerous books, including *The Freudian Body: Psychoanalysis and Art and Homos.*

Adam Phillips is a psychoanalyst, visiting professor in the Department of English at York University, the general editor of Penguin Modern Classics' Freud translations, and the author of twelve books, including *Going Sane* and *Side Effects.*

Back Cover Material

"In this fascinating and disturbing book, two writers with prose styles and intellectual styles that are at once famously identifiable and intimately personal celebrate the possibility of relationships that defy identity and undo personality. Braiding together brilliant psychoanalytic reflections on fiction and film, on the serial killer Jeffrey Dahmer and the invasion of Iraq, on suicidally unsafe sex and Socrates' theory of love, Bersani and Phillips at once dream of shattering the ego and, in their own distinct voices, display its miraculous, tragicomic persistence."

STEPHEN GREENBLATT, author of *Will in the World: How Shakespeare Became Shakespeare*

"This tremendous accomplishment showcases the talents of two agile, wonderfully erudite minds. As they weigh our desire for intimacy and explain why it so often fails, Bersani and Phillips grapple with issues as weighty as aggression and state-sanctioned violence. Every facet of the subject is handled with impressive care and intelligence. *Intimacies* is often lyrical, even occasionally elegiac, but for a book about impersonal narcissism I found it surprisingly poignant, personal, and affecting."

CHRISTOPHER LANE, author of *Shyness: How Normal Behavior Became a Sickness*

"*Intimacies* is a very incisive and gentle exchange between two writers who have thought and rethought psychoanalysis in powerful terms for contemporary culture. The dialogue enacts the kind of relationality it seeks to know, moving beyond the traditional narcissism of authorship, probing the important difference between being a psychological subject and finding a way to be present to another person. Psychoanalysis is moved beyond the theory of the ego and developmental norms, returned to primary questions of how and why pleasure is often at odds with self-preservation, and how such enduring tensions are presented in visual media, sexual practice, dialogue, and clinical exchange. Practiced here is an intimacy that explores the regions of impersonal coexistence where losing the self expands the capacity to love. This is a beautifully crafted book, one that underscores how the social life of the psyche is a matter of risk, wager, suspense, excitation, bodies, talk, and all manner of things both dangerous and sustaining."

JUDITHBUTLER, author of *Undoing Gender*

Books For ALL Kinds of Readers

At ReadHowYouWant we understand that one size does not fit all types of readers. Our innovative, patent pending technology allows us to design new formats to make reading easier and more enjoyable for you. This helps improve your speed of reading and your comprehension. Our EasyRead printed books have been optimized to improve word recognition, ease eye tracking by adjusting word and line spacing as well as minimizing hyphenation. Our EasyRead SuperLarge editions have been developed to make reading easier and more accessible for vision-impaired readers. We offer Braille and DAISY formats of our books and all popular E-Book formats.

We are continually introducing new formats based upon research and reader preferences. Visit our web-site to see all of our formats and learn how you can Personalize our books for yourself or as gifts. Sign up to Become A RHYW Registered Reader.

www.readhowyouwant.com

Printed in Great Britain
by Amazon

63471960R00084